The
Experience
of
Ultimate
Truth

The

Experience

of

Ultimate

Truth

MICHAEL GRAHAM

28 years of disciplined practice with India's
most respected gurus, leads to a surprising
conclusion.

Secunderabad

The Experience Of Ultimate Truth
by Michael Graham

Copyright © 2001 by Michael Graham
Originally published by U-TURN PRESS: www.youturnworks.com

First Indian edition 2003
ISBN 81-7362-478-X

All Scripture quotations, unless otherwise indicated, are taken from the *Holy Bible,* New International Version®. NIV® Copyright © 1973, 1978, 1984 by International Bible Society.

Published in India by
OM Books
P. O. Box 2014
Secunderabad 500003
Andhra Pradesh, India.

DEDICATION

To my dearest son Yogiraj
- a pleasure, an inspiration and a help always.

THE EXPERIENCE OF ULTIMATE TRUTH

MICHAEL GRAHAM

CONTENTS

Acknowledgement
Foreword
Introduction

Chapter	1	Uncommon Beginnings	17
Chapter	2	Meeting the Great Yogi	39
Chapter	3	Muktananda's Western Thrust	67
Chapter	4	Business, Reading & Practice	91
Chapter	5	A Leap into Full Service	105
Chapter	6	The Decision Principle	130
Chapter	7	The End Game Begins	141
Chapter	8	Big Surprises	175
Chapter	9	A New Beginning	199
Chapter	10	Reflections	209

ACKNOWLEDGEMENT

A great debt of gratitude goes to my friend Philip Johnson, without whose encouragement this story would not have been written.

His generous gift of time brought us together for one week over a computer where he diligently typed out the text as I scoured my memory and sought the most faithful way of recounting and wording the story.

FOREWORD

The book you are about to read is the spiritual autobiography of an ardent disciplined devotee, Michael Graham. He has a fascinating and compelling journey to share that straddles four continents, spanning over thirty years. Through his eyes you will be taken into the charismatic, intoxicating worlds of Hinduism and the human potential branch of 'New Age' style spirituality.

This is not a ho-hum, so what, who cares, take it or leave it story. Michael is distinguished as one who has rubbed shoulders with the leading gurus and teachers of our time. As he discloses, Michael was among the first three Western devotees of Swami Muktananda's Siddha Yoga. Michael's spiritual induction became a legendary illustration to others in the movement. He helped to organize one leg of Muktananda's first world tour in 1970. He would spend sixteen years in the movement, working in, or managing, the ashrams in Ganeshpuri, Miami, Los Angeles, New York and Melbourne.

However, Michael was not just involved in Siddha Yoga. He spent time with other leading gurus such as Bhagwan Shree Rajneesh (now known as Osho), Swami Rudrananda, Da Free John, U.G. Krishnamurti and H.W.L. Poonja. He also explored mind powers in Silva Mind Control, The Forum and *Avatar*. Michael met 'New Age' luminaries like Marilyn Ferguson and Ingo Swann, and was a friend of the esoteric writer Israel Regardie. He went on to become a successful mind power teacher in his own right, combining the best insights that he had found in both Hindu and Human Potential thought.

Michael's story winds its way across the decades and continents and brings us to a startling and amazing mystical experience that has transformed and empowered his entire being. His thirst for authentic spirituality was slaked in a dramatic and powerful encounter with the divine being who made our world. From that explosive moment, Michael has walked in a new direction, a spiritual discipline filled with grace and thanksgiving. He has some deep thoughts to share on what this means for him. He believes what he has discovered also has implications for those of us who are willing to listen.

You are in for a reader's feast, with many courses on the menu to digest and meditate on. As you read you may laugh a little, be dazzled at times, and even feel your feathers ruffled by some of the things Michael shares. You would expect nothing less than this from one who has trekked through so many spiritual disciplines. This is not just a spiritual travelogue of a lone pilgrim. There is an invitation to a banquet with the God who beckons us in love to taste and see.

Philip Johnson
Founder, New Age Mission
Lecturer, Alternative Spiritual Movements,
PTC & Morling Colleges, Sydney

INTRODUCTION

This life has been an uncommon one. I have met and lived with some of the most remarkable spiritual masters and gurus in both the East and West. Among the most extraordinary was Swami Muktananda, who later came to be known in the United States as the Guru's Guru. As the first Australian to have set foot in his Indian *ashram* in 1969, I lived to see the movement of Siddha Yoga expand to around a quarter of a million devotees with centers in forty six countries.

At the age of twenty-two I went to India to meet Swami Muktananda. I was told he was the great dispenser of grace. He could make possible, by effortless means, self-realization or enlightenment – the crowning promise of Hinduism. Indeed Muktananda's grace demonstrated itself to be a tantalizing phenomenon, amazing in all its manifestations. I was fascinated and gripped by what was to follow.

One balmy afternoon meditating on a tiger's skin on Muktananda's verandah, I was startled by the sensation of someone stroking my forehead and cheeks. I looked up, and there was the master blessing me with his touch, which was claimed to yield the beginning and the end of spiritual fulfillment. What followed soon after was a dramatic awakening that rendered spiritual practice spontaneous. I was hooked and in for the long haul. This was not the mere bread and butter variety of yoga or meditation commonly experienced with Indian spiritual teachers. This was *dunamis*, the Greek word from which we get the word 'dynamite'.

Muktananda was the primary tantalizer of my spiritual search for the next sixteen years of disciplined practice. However during this time, life led me onto the personal paths of Franklin Jones (a.k.a. Da Free John), Acharya Rajneesh, (who later became the world famous Osho), Baba Ram Dass, (a.k.a. Richard Alpert from Harvard and an associate of Timothy Leary), Anandamayi Ma, H. W. L. Poonja, U. G. Krishnamurti, and Swami Rudrananda, (known as Rudi). I later encountered Marilyn Ferguson (author of *The Aquarian Conspiracy*), Israel Regardie, Ingo Swann, both of whom became personal friends, and Harry Palmer, to name just a few. Each had their interesting features and contributed to my life experience along the way.

Where did all of this lead? What actually happened and what did I make of it? After all, I was on a quest for ultimate truth, fired by a zeal to find 'God', ignited by the promises of the Indian tradition. Encounters, adventures, marvels, disappointments and final fulfillment – that's the story. Perhaps as readers you might be able to identify with elements of my quest. My hope remains that by sharing this, the highways and byways of your own adventure may be illumined and more definitely honed.

1
UNCOMMON BEGINNINGS

'Standing at the front door was a three-year-old in diapers, holding his father's walking stick and smoking a cigarette.' This was the description of me by an amazed family friend, who years later assured me this was the truth. My father, being an avant-garde medical doctor and psychoanalyst, felt that the unbridled freedom of youth was the key to perfect integration. I was raised in this spirit, at least in my earliest days.

Both mother and father were remarkable people in their own right. My father was born in the mid-Pacific, on Ocean Island. His father was the doctor for the British Phosphate Company. At eighteen months of age, Dad came with his family to Australia. Tragically he was struck down with polio in the 1916 Sydney epidemic. Despite being seriously affected in both arms and legs, he rose through the medical ranks to become a psychiatrist and then one of the doyens of psychoanalysis in Australia. He was a kind and strong man of high integrity. He was loved and respected by many people.

My mother was born in Port Fairy in Victoria and came from a refined and well-educated family. Her mother was a school teacher and her father was the manager of the National Australia Bank. Mum was a great lover of beauty, spending the last forty years of her life as a painter and teacher of art. She would liberally quote from Shakespeare, Wordsworth, Shelley, Banjo Patterson or Omar Khayyam, in response to daily life situations. She was the most spontaneous person I have known. She was delightful and free of affectation, and was a wonderful listener without the slightest wavering of attention. However, particularly in the earliest years of my life, she was not so stable. According to all accounts, my parents had a happy marriage before I was born. Birth and post-partum depression knocked Mum around and when I was three she went to bed for a year. Perhaps she was Australia's first victim of Chronic Fatigue Syndrome.

My mother's decline and her dysfunction, and her growing unreasonableness, taxed my father's natural forbearance to the limits. Finally things snapped in a huge marriage dissolution with Mum's family, which included a lawyer and a judge, and Dad's family of four doctors, seriously estranged from each other. Surely I remember some hard times, and psychologists would love to ascribe the worst to all this. But alas for them I was as I was, I am as I am, and all remained well.

At the age of seven, after some dust had settled following the divorce, I was sent to the elite Geelong Grammar Boarding School – the one to which Prince Charles was later sent. Here I spent the next ten years of my life until aged eighteen. The early years started off grimly. Perhaps it was like a soft form of something Charles Dickens wrote about. As I grew older, greater freedoms were given and I was consumed by the enjoyment of sport, Australian Rules Football, athletics, hurdling, and above all my greatest love, gymnastics. The academics were incidental. I reached my peak at eleven, topping a class. From then on I became academically more mediocre, but sometimes topped my Latin class. I nearly made it to a classical education, but not quite.

During this time I was given the three bears version of Christianity. My first memory of the Christian teaching, since Mum and Dad were not the least bit interested in this, was being asked at school to conform to the character of Christ. I can remember being intrigued by this, but realized it was quite impossible. Fifteen minutes of chapel each day, encultured me to an appreciation of Christian aesthetics – the hymns, King James' English, the loveliness of it all. This appreciation came out later. At the time it was deadly boring.

My weak interest in Christianity peaked while attending Geelong Grammar's well-renowned Timbertop school year in the mountains. During my Christian confirmation I was touched on the forehead by the bishop and had my first exceedingly small spiritual experience. It was enough for me to think 'Ooh what was that?' Promptly I forgot about it and only resorted to prayer some months later when I was picked on by an oafish French teacher. He took exception to my placing a huge log under the back wheel of his four-wheel-drive Land Rover. This had caused him to spend several minutes in deep confusion as to why the machine wouldn't move forward as ten boys sat muffling their laughter in the back. For this mischief he came down on me like a ton of bricks. He vilified my name in every class he taught for the next three weeks. Much oppressed I did a bit of praying to get some relief. That was the extent of my Christianity.

Around this time my intellect began to wake up. An inquiry began, bringing into question what life was all about. My father had a mild interest in mysticism. Some of the books on the shelf of his large library reflected this. After pulling a few of them down and inspecting their argument, I began to be deeply impressed by the promises of yoga. This was not particularly the yoga of the toe-touching variety, though I did start out with this, wanting to increase my athletic capacities. It was rather the spirituality of it all that captivated me — the promise of enlightenment or self-realization, total freedom and the end of all suffering. It sounded seriously interesting to me. Where do I sign? So it was from this recognition that the spiritual quest began. It was in earnest and placed itself at center stage of my life.

At the time life wasn't easy, mainly because I couldn't find a vocation that strongly interested me. In the absence of this clarity perhaps, I gravitated to an interest in self-development, the *summum bonum* of which would have been the fulfillment of the yogic promise.

Meanwhile, Dad, always keen to be helpful, and a champion of psychoanalysis, suggested I undergo psychoanalysis. It was supposed to bring me to a level of clarity and life direction that was a sound thing for any young man to possess. Dad was a fair dinkum psychoanalyst. He was not one of the weird variety that might be caricatured in movies. He was a refined and mature man who kept his psychological thinking and talk within the bounds of his consulting room. He himself had undergone, as part of the mandatory training for a psychoanalyst, four years of psychoanalysis as a 'patient'. Here I was following his footsteps, at least to this degree. As it turned out for me the psychoanalytical experience was a joke. It was ineffectual and I can fairly say that I derived absolutely nothing from it. Nothing. I think poor Dad blamed himself for choosing, as he realized later, an incompetent psychoanalyst to be my man. Anyway, over the years I did have further experiential brushes with the psychological paradigm, and to this day have found it moribund and wanting.

At the same time I had been practising *Hatha Yoga*

and breath control, along with attempts to meditate. Being a gymnast, most postures of *Hatha Yoga* were a piece of cake. I was the apple of my Indian teacher's eye, being able to perform with ease the exercises some fellow students found difficult to perfect. But the meditation bit had me stumped. For the life of me, every attempt I made to reach a state of quiescence had the reverse effect. Each time I tried it, I ended up frustrated and in knots. But the promise was still there and I wasn't about to give up. I decided, at the recommendation of my Melbourne Indian teacher, to go and check out the greatest contemporary Indian guru and yogi of all time, Swami Muktananda.

It was to take me three years to make this trip. In the meantime I had my first intimations of spirituality through nature during an adventure in the Central Australian Desert.

At age twenty-one I read in a daily newspaper of a proposed expedition to find Lasseter's Reef. Lasseter had been a prospector with some civil engineering training who had discovered an exceedingly rich vein of gold near the remote Petermann Ranges in the Central Australian Desert.

On July 21 1929, with much publicity, he set out on a well-equipped and costly expedition to rediscover and exploit the find. Lasseter and his chief companion perished of hunger and exposure after going it alone on camels after the expedition's four-wheel drive trucks had bogged and the aircrafts that served them had crashed. He limped on in the care of aboriginal nomads after his friend died, and before he himself perished.

The story is one of the most absorbingly interesting and poignant tales of Australian exploration. There have been many attempts to decipher the where-abouts of the reef from Lasseter's maps which he had buried in a cave along with his diary. It contained his last words to his wife and an account of all that he had been through.

In the 1980s even the Australian Army assisted one hopeful group in searching for the reef as a military logistics exercise.

Our particular expedition set out, led by Neville Harding, a former Lord Mayor of Sydney. He had attempted and failed to find the reef some ten years earlier. This time he had done more research and was fully equipped with three four-wheel-drive Land Rovers, a Second World War Blitz Wagon and a single engine aircraft.

Fascinated by the prospect of joining this expedition, I phoned up from Melbourne offering my services as a driver. Neville Harding and I got along well on the phone. He suggested I come up to Sydney and see him. I took an enthusiastic dash up there and was hired. Filmed on television on March 27 1967, our three Land Rovers made a grand exit from Sydney with me at the wheel of one of them. We made it to Alice Springs right in the center of Australia, part of the journey being over an arduous one thousand miles of rutted dirt road starting at Port Augusta in South Australia. As we waited in the Alice, a documentary crew flew in and the Blitz Wagon rumbled in from Darwin in the far north. We waited patiently for six days for our delayed leader to fly in from Sydney.

The expedition members and equipment finally gathered and we took off along the dirt road to Ayers Rock (now named Uluru). The Rock is an exquisite monolith, the biggest in the world, sitting right in the dead heart of Australia.

There were virtually no tourists in those days. A dirt air-strip serviced the Rock, with a pile of forty-four gallon drums at one end to replenish the fuel of the light aircraft that landed. I walked to the top of the Rock and then ran down again enjoying the feat of braking as I descended with all my wits about me. A fall down that sand-papery surface to hit bottom would leave anyone a sorry dead mess. For the next three days my legs were like rubber, barely able to support me from the battering they took from the enjoyable full speed descent.

About fifty miles past the Rock, on our way into the dead heart of nowhere, the Blitz Wagon broke an axle. That stopped us. We radioed the Alice and the pilot flew in a replacement axle, hurling it from the window as his plane swept low.

Miles on, upon reaching the Docker River we left the sandy track near the spot where Lasseter had buried his map in a cave. From there we bashed our way through the mulga scrub and across brilliant red sandy soil towards a destination only Neville our leader knew.

The country was exquisite. The peculiar redness of the soil was not to be believed – the purple wild flowers and the colors playing on the rocks in the late afternoon sun – oh my goodness, how glorious! This beauty brought me to my knees. I had never seen anything like it, nor had I known absolute silence before. From this I would hang on the brink of an apperception of nature's mysterious beauty. There was a driving frustration in it, not unlike having something on the tip of one's tongue and its not coming. Something was on the other side of this beauty. It baited me, beckoning me to know it. Alas, I could not quite cross the bridge over which I was being called. Nightly as I lay beneath the brilliant canopy of stars, I was affected in the same way. Never before had I come as close to 'breakthrough' as a guest of nature.

It was in those days that I had begun to think it a trifle unlikely that the exactness and genius of the creation was the product of a flukish coming together of a bunch of elemental gases.

It was tiring to be lurched around all day over trackless ground. When necessary we took it in turns to be out in front of the Land Rovers, clearing the way of Mulga wood. The seventy-two year old Neville was out there, keeping up as well as anyone. Repeatedly we were repairing punctures as the rock hard Mulga wood splinters would pierce our tires. One day we had eighteen punctures, each of which had to be manually repaired. The Blitz Wagon however, had such thick ply tires, that it plowed over the wood unaffected. I loved it when I had a shot at driving that thing with all its gears, despite having to put up with suffocating exhaust fumes entering the cabin.

Finally we reached our base camp, beauty all about us. By now I had grown to know Neville better. Among other things he was a quasi-spiritualist and an astrologer. He had more in common with me than with most of the other conventional chaps. So most often I was the one to drive his lead Land Rover.

After dark one evening he said to me, 'Let's go'. The two of us took off alone in the Land Rover to I don't know where. It seemed as though he was trying to figure something out. We talked and looked at the stars, all the while my wondering 'Where on earth are we?' 'How will we find our way back to camp?' To my amazement however, it was never any trouble to Neville. He told me that he navigated by the stars.

At base camp we had to build an airstrip. As best we could, we smoothed out a stretch of the desert, clearing away some Mulga wood obstructions. We thought our job looked pretty good so we radioed the pilot to fly in. As he swooped low to check out his new landing strip he let out a ream of Aussie expletives complaining that he didn't fancy getting killed on that strip as we scrambled to improve it as he circled.

Along with some supplies, he had flown in with a dowser; a 'mystic' pal of Neville's who had a novel sensing device to help us dowse for gold as a supplement to Neville's carefully worked out conventional reckonings. I can remember bouncing our way along the ridges for several days of searching and hearing our dowsing mate say, 'There ain't no #$#*!!* gold here Nev'. But we did, however, find lead, copper and zinc as assays back in Sydney confirmed.

All the while this adventure was being professionally filmed by a documentary crew that had accompanied us. The film produced was called *The Die Hard: The Legend of Lasseter*. It was narrated by the British film star James Mason and won the Australian Film Industry award for the best documentary shown at the Melbourne Film Festival in 1970. We were yet another expedition that failed to find the gold. People still look for it today.

We in our Land Rovers finally made it back to Sydney via Tennant Creek in the Northern Territory and Mount Isa and Brisbane in Queensland.

But this great trek was to take place all over again. This time it was with just three of us in one vehicle: Jack Smith, a bush wacker with savvy; Graeme Corneliusen, a rice farmer from Leeton, New South Wales; and me. Our mission was to stake the claim; to secure the find of copper, lead and zinc.

Again we arrived in the dead heart; three people all alone, hundreds of miles from another soul, enveloped by the silence and beauty. Again, an illuminating encounter with nature at her best.

Prevailing upon my companions from shooting every red kangaroo in sight and having the front suspension torn out of our vehicle by ploughing into a rabbit warren, made it a trip to remember indeed. We limped back into Ayers Rock with our torn front suspension trussed up with cable wire and with our last tire flapping from being ripped apart by Mulga wood.

With illustrations, photos and maps, the original story of Lasseter is wonderfully told by Ion Idriess in his book *Lasseter's Last Ride*.

Now back in Melbourne I returned to my yogic practices and was soon to launch off to India to find my guru-to-be, Swami Muktananda. This was 1968.

At this time Swami Muktananda was entirely unknown in the West.

Just as an interesting note, for the next twenty five years my mother and father followed me into everything I did, coming to India and doing the trainings and courses I recommended. For a medical doctor and a nurse, this was somewhat unusual. Or at least I thought so at the time and so did others. I was considered lucky to have such open-minded parents.

So I set out with two others, with motorcycles, bound for London via Sri Lanka (Ceylon) and India. Triumphantly we left on the big ship *Orsova*. We were photographed on the wharf by the *Melbourne Herald* newspaper with a big splash picture and editorial on these young world adventurers. At the time the overland trip to Europe through Asia was not the sort of thing every Joe was doing.

We disembarked in Colombo and circumnavigated the island of Sri Lanka on our motorcycles. It was beautiful indeed. The hills at Kandy, the white sand beaches, the government rest houses, where we young westerners on a budget could yet afford to be served tea by the sea by a uniformed Ceylonese, deferring as one once would, to the British Raj. Here I was gypped on a gem deal that caused a stir. The dealer was dragged from two hundred kilometers away by the Tourist Commission to give account for his chicanery. I got my few dollars back. And can you believe it, I was then gypped again by the fellow who gave the tip off that I had originally been gypped. I was young and naive.

So off we went to the southern tip of India and right up through the center of the country. We passed through blisteringly hot plains into the relief of the hill stations and onwards. I thought the food was terrible. I mostly lived on bananas and chapattis, and all my German friend Herbert could think of was where he was going to find his next beer to kill the heat. This bloke was not strongly interested in spirituality or ashram life. The third motorcyclist was Hilly; a lovely Catholic girl. She was very giving, always relinquishing the last morsel on her plate to either of us who had finished our food and was looking around for more.

Later on I was to appreciate Indian cuisine as the

most delectable of all. I had many trips to India and an aggregate of four years in the country, becoming more and more delighted with many of the elements that country had to offer.

So there I was at the gateway of India in Bombay, astride my motorcycle, Swami Muktananda's address in hand. He was only fifty miles north. The question was – would I or wouldn't I go? The others certainly weren't keen and I'd become jaded by the yogic scene by my failure to meditate successfully. So I put off my divine encounter and decided to make my way overland to London.

As we proceeded up through India by motorcycle, the culture shock of the Indian style of doing things became difficult to us westerners. The magnificence of Srinigar in Kashmir with its Dal lake surrounded by snow-capped mountains came as something of a relief as we were served English roast dinners on our commodious houseboat.

Before reaching Kashmir we had all relinquished our bikes. My pretty Honda Street Scrambler, that drew such delighted attention in Indian villages, was shipped back to Australia along with Hilly's Yamaha. My German friend's clunker was surrendered to customs as it was worth less than the cost of shipping. So we proceeded through Pakistan, a slightly 'martial' version of India – due to Islamic influence – and on to Kabul in Afghanistan.

What a relief Afghanistan was, different again and more relaxing to be in. Here a serious adventure began. We were stuck. We were unable to leave Afghanistan by land because of a cholera scare, and were not willing to fly out via Russia because we didn't want to spend the money.

By now Hilly and Herbert had gone well in advance of me to Europe and I was camped amongst a number of others on the Khaga Dam, some thirty miles north of Kabul, waiting with other frustrated westerners for clearance to enter Iran.

The wait was maddening because we simply had no idea when and if this clearance would come. Frustrated by a complete lack of information, a group of us 'stormed' the Iranian Embassy in Kabul sending delegations in to demand clearance. Meanwhile our companions demonstrated outside, being courteously bridled by very simple ill-clad policemen whose job it was to maintain order. Their officers on the other hand were beautifully dressed in a style reminiscent of the slickness of the Second World War German military. It was a strange contrast. Our storming had got us nowhere.

Some days later an Australian wild man, shortish, wiry, with a large bushy beard (we'll call him Rob for discretion's sake), pulled up at the lake and yelled out at us 'Does anyone here want to buy a seat to Istanbul?' He ran an old tour bus between London and Kathmandu via Kabul. At forty dollars it seemed like a good deal. Besides, Rob said he knew the ropes and could navigate this problem better than we could alone. We found ourselves queued up on the Afghani-Iranian border awaiting our turn to enter. This was taking time as Iranian doctors were examining all entrants, particularly dallying with the young western women. We were stopped at that border for three days. There were probably twenty-five of us on the bus and lots of other vehicles waiting. Hourly, Rob was getting madder and madder. We found out later that he loathed Iranians.

Two years earlier, after a row over the tip with an Iranian tea shop owner, his bus was drained of oil at midnight. It was only half an hour down the road next day that the engine of his bus seized up leaving him stranded in Iran with a busload of paying customers. Rob hated Iranians thereafter. His attitude started to infect the whole bus. Indeed cultural differences were marked. Iranians turned out to be as different to Afghanis, as Afghanis were to Indians and Pakistanis. Every young western woman was leered at, pinched or buffeted on the streets of Teheran several times per day. This was not an exaggeration. Such a thing was most unlikely to

31

happen in the other surrounding countries that we had passed through.

Finally as our bus waited in line to cross the border, Rob snapped. And much to our dismay we took off without permission into a short stretch of no-man's-land between Afghanistan and Iran. The next thing we knew there was a 1950s Studebaker sedan filled with gun-toting soldiers chasing the bus tooting their horn. We quietly invited Rob to stop. He let out an expletive and accelerated. This wasn't funny. Sluicing about in the mud the Studebaker finally got past the bus by angling across our bows and forcing us to stop. The soldiers leapt out. Four of them stood outside the bus lined up as though on a parade ground while their boss walked through the bus in a state of muffled fury. Now we were doubly stuck. We couldn't go back into Afghanistan nor could we proceed into Iran. Stuck another two days in no-man's-land, and all we had on board was dry Afghani bread. We had to muster all the diplomacy possible to persuade the Iranians to bring us water while we waited to be cleared. This was all nerve-racking, especially as Rob's behavior seemed uncontrollable and there was no-one in our party willing to deal with him. The role fell to me to sit up front ready to quadruple check him if his behavior threatened to get us into deadly trouble.

Thinking we were over the worst, worse was to

come. As the sun set on the second day the Iranians finally called us to Quarantine. The medicos did their physical inspections as we waited. It came time for our vaccination certificates to be inspected. By this time we were back on the bus and a friendly Iranian Quarantine official informed Rob that he, the official, our vaccination certificates and us, were to drive one mile for the appropriate bureaucratic checking of our health documents. Rob flatly refused to go one inch out of his way. There was a screaming match and the official got off the bus with all our certificates in his hand. Rob fired up the Gardener diesel and off we went.

We couldn't believe it. Here we were barreling down the road in a foreign country without our compulsory vaccination certificates, leaving behind a bunch of steaming Iranian officials back on the border. A debate followed. There was no way we westerners were going to have another vaccination just because Rob wasn't willing to do the right thing. In the middle of our concerned conversation we were by now several miles from the border. I was sitting in the front seat and noticed several hundred yards ahead two men holding a heavy chain across the road. Obviously the Iranian officials had phoned ahead and told the police to stop us. Did Rob stop? Forget it. Much to my dismay he slammed the diesel into third gear and accelerated. Sixty seconds later there was a terrible thwanging sound as our bus ploughed through the chain held by the two hapless policemen on either side of the road. At this point we were scared. What were these Iranians going to do with us? This was the era of the Shah's notorious 'Savak' police. To this day I can barely believe it. That was the last we heard of the whole saga. We were home free.

Despite a swollen Iranian river crossing that came within an ace of Rob losing his second bus, he only gave us one more cause for alarm. During a ten minute stop in a village, he had asked us to be back to the bus precisely on time. Some chap failed to show. Unperturbed, Rob took off. It was in the middle of nowhere and the chap's passport and gear were on board. It took me ten minutes to persuade Rob to stop. He absolutely refused to turn back to pick up the abandoned man. A volunteer got off the bus and caught a cart back into town. He found the poor bloke walking around in a daze in the middle of the town square.

We finally got to Istanbul. I then made my way down the coast of Turkey to Ephesus and crossed to the beautiful island of Rhodes by fishing boat where I spent an enchanting week in the village of Lyndos.

In some ways the four month trip to Europe had been long and tedious. I hadn't been easily captivated by the sights. Hiring motor scooters on

Rhodes put a smile back on my face. By now I was travelling with two Canadians. I was riding one motor scooter, they on another. We set out for Lyndos together and I was puzzled by their having disappeared from behind me. Patiently I waited for ten minutes and then turned back to see what might have happened. They'd ridden over a small cliff. The first I knew of it was from one of them, who kneeling in a bullock cart, stammered out that they'd come to grief. He was drenched in blood. It was an awful sight. Then a car sped past, apparently containing my other friend. He was unmarked but had broken his back though not to the point of paralysis. After a couple of days in hospital, my bloodied friend was cheerfully walking about. He'd experienced multiple lacerations, while the other one was flown out to Canada in a heavy-looking cast. Thankfully he recovered.

By boat, I then made my way across to Crete and on to Athens, through Corfu to Brindisi on the east coast of Italy. If only the ice cream wasn't so expensive. It was delicious and I could have lived on it. I made my way across to Rome and up through Florence to Venice. While hitch-hiking from there, an accommodating priest and his acolyte picked me out of the rain and took me up through Austria all the way to Remscheid in Germany. Their hospitality was touching, except for their insistence that I drink the odd beer. At that time I considered beer one of the foulest tasting drinks imaginable. Amsterdam was next. Then I purchased a student flight to London, where an adventure began that ripened me for a zealous return to partake of the Eastern spiritual promise.

In London I got a £6.00 per week job as a lifeguard at an indoor swimming pool. Later I secured a job at Australia House, where I was doing considerably better at £13.00 a week. Within a week I was in total overwhelm. Some chap was given only one week to fill me in on a complicated job ordering spare parts for helicopters and jets from all over Europe for the Australian armed forces. I had visions of everything dropping out of the sky through my not getting it right. All efforts to get correctly grooved-in failed, so I quit and went off skiing in Austria for two weeks.

During my London time, a girlfriend disappointment and a business enterprise that fell over, readied me for the yogic way of exclusive focus on the spiritual path, free from any materialistic entanglements. Disposed in this way, I took off for India in early 1969, ripe for meeting Swami Muktananda.

2
MEETING THE GREAT YOGI

This was unknown territory. I headed for the ashram in Ganeshpuri which is eighty kilometers north of Bombay (now Mumbai), not having any idea what to expect. I had never seen a picture of Muktananda nor could I pronounce his name. When I arrived there Muktananda was not home. All around the walls of the ashram were large photographs of a man I assumed was Muktananda. As it turned out, these were pictures of Muktananda's own guru, Bhagawan Nityananda, a renowned ascetic yogi, an *avadhut*, the title referring to one who is unconstrained by social conventions. Two days after my arrival, the moment of meeting came. Excitedly, with twenty Indians I waited out the front of the ashram for his arrival. There were only three of us westerners. One was a tall young Englishman by the name of Michael Goldsmith, the other an American named Larry Stroup.

The first sign of Muktananda's arrival was the sounding of a claxon horn. Up pulled a blue 1962 Mercedes-Benz, and out stepped a handsome sixty year old dressed in brilliant orange silk robes and wearing sunglasses. He had a commanding air about him, and the level of respect and devotion he elicited was extraordinary and unfamiliar to me. He strode past, glancing in my direction as he went, with devotees dropping at his feet in gestures of full prostration. And as he moved he lightly tapped them with his feet, saying 'Look out, look out this is a fast train!' (Someone translated this for me afterwards). With a white beard, he certainly didn't fit the picture-book image of the holy man dispensing blessings, wearing a smile of transcendental beatitude. But Muktananda did not disappoint. I could see he was extraordinary from the moment I laid eyes on him – no lightweight.

A couple of days later I had a chance to meet him personally and tell him that my meditation was no good. I explained I had come all the way from abroad to have it fixed. He said, through his translator, 'Don't worry. Everything will be fine.' I carried on for a week doing my characteristic forceful, techniquey meditation, making an effort and getting nowhere.

I sat meditating all alone late one afternoon, sitting on a real tiger's skin. This was in the verandah meditation room, which surrounded Muktananda's quarters. Suddenly I was startled by someone stroking me across both cheeks and across the forehead. I looked up and there was Muktananda standing over me. I was delighted and somewhat in awe. This over, he turned on his heels and left. I had received 'the touch' of the guru, the eminent one. This touch constituted the transmission of divine energy from the Guru to the disciple. It's called *Shaktipat*. Each day thereafter Muktananda would ask me, in English mind you, 'Good meditation?' And I would simply reply, 'No Baba'. Each day he would repeat the question and each time I had to report that nothing was happening. It's quite funny, but I actually became irritated by his incessant inquiry because I was expecting something to happen and so was he. Nothing was forthcoming.

Two weeks after his touch, I was sitting quietly, and all of a sudden my body began to sway. Fascinated, I allowed it to continue and then immediately stopped it. I was altogether curious that this bodily movement would be taking place all on its own. I'd bring it into check and give over in an experimental manner. It was as though I were researching a new phenomenon.

Each day thereafter the scope and intensity of this gyrating circular motion of the body would increase. It was nothing less than amazing. Never before had my body moved without my volition. I was doubly fascinated as the intensity of these bodily movements increased. As it went on I remained wholly in possession of my wits.

I remember one day when a young Indian boy was squinting through the bamboo blinds watching this bizarre activity. I had a grin on my face from ear to

39

ear. Later the young boy asked me, 'Were you in ecstasy?' I told him the grin had nothing to do with ecstasy. I was just totally amazed at what was going on and amused by it.

A week or so later, a chap by the name of Don Mason, who had just arrived from Canada, sat down and meditated with me on the verandah. This meditation room was filled with exotic leopard, tiger and deer skins, all provided for the meditator's yogic comfort. As we were meditating together Don decided to repeat the famous twenty-third Psalm from the Bible, beginning, 'The Lord is my shepherd, I shall not want.' This Psalm was familiar to me. I was profoundly moved by its beauty. At that moment of being most deeply touched there was a terrific explosion of energy within me, and the degree of the awakening I received from Muktananda intensified tenfold. I was flung to the floor and started crawling my way across the meditation room making a sound like a ferocious lion. It was devastatingly powerful and realistic, not as any ham actor could do. I was agog. This was unbelievable. The Canadian across from me was beside himself with fear. He'd never seen anything like this in his whole life. All he knew to do was to repeat the *mantra* 'Guru Om, Guru Om' aloud, trying vainly to settle down the situation. All this while I was as fascinated and amazed as he was afraid. In the next moment I was lifted to my feet with the energy and strength of ten men pulsing through me. I was swept to the door of the meditation room in the grip of this powerful energy. The ashram dogs – aggressive and sullen mutts at the best of times – must have sensed something. At the sight of me they started to bark and go down on their forepaws and back off. The next thing I knew I was running through the lower ashram garden on my way to the paddy fields, which at this time of year were dry blocks of broken earth.

I began to sprint across these fields. Had I done it volitionally I would have probably broken both ankles in sixteen places. But such was the intelligence that moved me that I came to no harm. Still under the influence of this awakening I found myself running toward the wall surrounding the lower ashram garden. It seemed to me about eight feet tall and I vaulted it with unfamiliar athletic prowess, all under the influence of this energy which is called *shakti*. At this time there were very few people in the ashram as Muktananda had left for the hill station of Mahabaleshwara to write his autobiography, *The Play of Consciousness*, which described his spiritual experiences. The word was getting around among the few that had remained that this Australian chap was having an amazing experience. As I moved I noticed faces peeping out from many corners.

Needless to say I was thrilled. The promise of the divine awakening within me had occurred in no uncertain terms. It was explosive, dynamic, palpable. It was to be surrendered to, not resisted. This, it is said, was the awakening of divine grace. It comes through the gift of the guru, through whose power the intelligence of the life force itself is awakened to bring a person to the state of God or Self-realization. The process of its being awakened by the Guru is called *shaktipat*. Twenty five years afterwards regarding this I wrote:

'Shakitpat is a supremely beneficent awakening. This entirely spontaneous and dynamic process automatically expunges a being of all past impressions that have stultified awareness. In this way it spontaneously draws one into an experiential penetration of one's true nature, opening up new levels of experience, peace, joy and spiritual union.

In contrast to the spontaneous way for spiritual reintegration, all man-made or mind-born prescriptions for spiritual enlightenment, no matter how sophisticated or clever, are fraught with the limitations of the ego (limited self) of which they are a product. This Divine Action suffers no such limitations. The Absolute (guru) becomes one's guide and the same supreme intelligence that turns a seed into a flower and keeps the planets on their axes, orients itself towards the spiritual unfoldment of the individual. This wasn't *precisely* Muktananda's take on it, but this is how I saw it years later.'

This awakening distinguished itself from common forms of yoga and meditation by being spontaneous, vibrant and charismatic. It was non-volitional. The attitude the aspirant was to have was to place him or herself in obedience under the authority of the guru and surrender to this awakened inner transformative force, which in those yet 'uninitiated' remained latent and unawakened. The special gift of the perfected spiritual master of this particular lineage, was to be able to awaken this force. The awakening rendered the spiritual journey natural and effortless.

From the day of this dramatic intensifying of my awakening, whenever I gave over to its workings, all sorts of spontaneous experiences occurred. There were intense breathing rhythms, dynamically and perfectly executed Hatha Yogic postures done entirely under the volition of the *shakti* energy, while the practitioner looked on in amazement. Utterances came forth, the sounds of animals and birds, so realistic without any volitional participation from the aspirant. There were moments of perfect quiescence, of peace and stillness, and in the next moment hysterical laughter or crying attendant to nothing funny or sad. There was ordered classical like dancing, speaking in tongues, swaying and juddering of the body and hopping about the floor like a frog, the seeing of lights of different colors, even journeys out of the body. This is to name but a few of the broad range of experiences typical of this awakening.

Singularly the most impressive thing about all this was that it took place independent of any additions or interferences from the aspirant. In fact it was very important to me in particular, not to add or subtract even the slightest bit to the experience. To preserve my intellectual integrity I had to vigilantly guard against any imaginings or additions of my own making.

This process went on for years. Each day, I simply gave over to it. The giving over in itself was remarkable. Sometimes the force would begin to work within me even before I had time to form the words or the thought 'to give over'. Between the intention and the thought the thing had already begun. And it could be as easily halted as it could be given over to. No hysteria, hypnosis or vain imaginings were involved as regards this phenomena.

Well you can imagine, I was delighted beyond measure. It was happening; the show was on the road. My enlightenment was assured as a gift of this grace. One would be enlightened within six, nine or twelve years, as Muktananda used to say.

Muktananda was delighted by the intensity of my awakening. News of this intensity reached him in Mahabaleshwara and so enamoured was he of it, that for the next thirteen years he cited many aspects of my experience with delight, as a demonstration of the dynamics of this awakening. In the last Siddha Yoga Intensive Program in India, held at the Taj Mahal Hotel before he died in 1982, he talked about the awakening experienced by 'the Australian businessman'. He used to laugh and say that not even ten men could have held me down. His own awakening earlier in his own spiritual journey had begun with similar intensity.

Muktananda had become a guru of great influence. He was able to be the agent of the precipitation of this awakening because he had received the same from his guru Bhagawan Nityananda back in 1947. Muktananda described the experiences of his own awakening in his autobiography *Play of Consciousness*. After assiduously giving himself over to this divine grace for six hours a day, over nine years; having total faith in his guru, and living a rigorous spiritual life of devotion to God, Muktananda's final fulfillment was supposed to have occurred. Voilà, enlightenment. Voilà, now the perfected being. Voilà, now the one who would be the instrument of enlightenment for others. Apparently Muktananda's guru, Bhagawan Nityananda, acknowledged and celebrated his final fulfillment, and passed, albeit unofficially, the mantle of the lineage onto him.

The spiritual lineage of Muktananada is known as Siddha Yoga. The word 'Siddha' means 'perfected being' and the word 'Yoga' means 'union with God' or being 'yoked' to God. So this yoga is the yoga that takes place through the grace of the perfected being. And of course the word 'grace' engenders the notion of a gift. This was attractive to me because it is a far cry from the grinding self-willed effort of any form of yoga that may not incorporate the palpable addition of grace. Muktananda was a guru *par excellence* from the Indian tradition. He was later to be known in America as the 'Guru's Guru'. Even Maharishi Mahesh Yogi of Transcendental Meditation fame admired him and invited him to be the spiritual adviser to his World Government concept.

According to one authority the word 'guru' is an ancient Sanskrit word meaning 'weighty' as in powerful or authoritative. There are four types of gurus in the Indian tradition. The foremost is the incarnation of God himself. Lord Krishna is an example. The second rank is the human being, who by virtue of grace bestowed and self-effort, has come to be unified with God. The third is a preceptor or dispenser of teachings and techniques. The fourth could be a teacher of any sort, including your parents. Muktananda could be considered to be one of the second highest rank. He ascribed his fulfillment exclusively to the divine grace of his guru Bhagawan Nityananda.

In the Indian spiritual tradition it is believed that we are all divine. The problem is that we are not experientially aware of it. We are encased in layers of stultifying influences or *karmas* that entrap us within an ever-lasting cycle of illusion (*maya*) and suffering.

Before we can recognize our true nature, the path must be cleared by erasing *karmas*. This deletion takes place by divine grace of the guru with the co-operation of total faith in the master. Discipline, service, devotion and discernment on the part of the aspirant are required. The awakening described above is supposed to burn up 'all the impurities' or obstacles which stand in the way of recognizing our true divine nature. So the action of this awakening supposedly purifies the whole being on the levels of soul, mind, emotions, will and body. This spiritual crud is supposedly caked within 72,000 channels of energy that flow throughout the five existing 'bodily' sheaths that 'encase' pure consciousness.

Muktananda having become a monk at fifteen, was discipled in the basic and familiar Hindu traditions particularly those of *Vedanta* and Yoga. By the way, the yoga we practise in the West most commonly is called *Hatha Yoga*. It is one of about fourteen types and considered the lowest of all. Interestingly enough, nothing from Muktananda's experience or reading, nor from his traversing India on foot three times, meeting many of the great sages of the day, prepared him for the nature of the awakening he was to get from Bhagawan Nityananda. When he received it he thought he was going mad, just as you may have thought I was, from my description above.

In Muktananda's case, as providence had it, he spotted a book lying open at a page that described what he was going through. This book was written in the 1930s by an obscure yogi who had been given the same awakening. Relieved, Muktananda now knew that these manifestations were a blessing, not a malfunction and continued his discipleship under Bhagawan Nityananda, albeit away from his physical presence for many years that followed.

A point worth making here is that Muktananda called this awakening, 'the awakening of the *Kundalini*!' The word *Kundalini* literally means 'serpent power'. It is the cosmic energy that lies dormant at the bottom of the spine that when awakened rises up through a series of energy centers (*chakras*) until it reaches and 'merges with God' in the crown of the head. Surely the awakening described included the *Kundalini*, but I believe, for many reasons that it was broader and more comprehensive. In fact many of Muktananda's devotees, who had wide-ranging dynamic spiritual experiences, often had no experiences associated with the locus of the spine at all. It lay beyond the scope of the classical explanations on this subject of *Kundalini* found in convoluted tomes such as *The Serpent Power,* written by Sir John Woodroffe at the end of the nineteenth century, and beyond any of the many books written on *Kundalini* by western 'dreamers'.

If this had been classic *Kundalini* that Muktananda had been experiencing, he would have seen recognizable descriptions detailed in scripture. Being an experienced and well-schooled yogi before he met Bhagawan Nityananda, he would not have been alarmed and dismayed at his awakening, but delighted. Such was not the case. Nothing had prepared him for the unusualness of these manifestations. So it's likely we are talking about an interesting 'new' phenomenon here.

There are many different energetic phenomena in the cosmic arena. Three of these are of the same genre and are almost identical. One was a burgeoning that sprang forth spearheaded by Muktananda (a Hindu) beginning in 1947 out of India. Another emerged through Pak Subuh (a Muslim) around the same time out of Indonesia. And there was yet another which came to be known as the 'Toronto blessing' which appeared in Christian Pentecostal circles in 1995. Each of these awakenings is non-volitional and is characterized by a similar range of spontaneous body movements and postures, unusual breathing, utterances and interior states, etc. that are far more comprehensive in scope than other genres of energetic phenomena.

In Siddha Yoga the excesses of the awakening have been 'discouraged' since the early 1970s for reasons of public decorum. Muktananda encouraged those who had extreme manifestations to go and allow them to happen in the privacy of their own homes.

Thus tantalized I applied myself to Muktananda's way for the next thirteen years up until his death in October 1982.

At the time of my first visit to the ashram in 1969, I was sufficiently marveled to spend five and a half months there. My father visited at that time. Muktananda was kind and gracious to him. Baba exclaimed when he met my father, 'Ah, the face of a philosopher.'

This ashram life was disciplined and rigorous. We would arise at 3.30 am and do ninety minutes of meditation. In the case of those who had the awakening they would be 'given over'. In the case of those who lived in hope, they would be repeating the *mantra* expecting the first stirrings of experience. It was an utterly experience-based spiritual system. Spiritual progress was predicated on spiritual experiences – on phenomena. Things weren't looking good if you were experience-free. In those days Baba would do all in his power to spark those few who seemed immune to the awakening.

After meditation tea was served, followed by the chanting of the *Bhagavad-Gita* for one and a half hours. Phew. This was tedious, especially as we few foreigners' had to sit through the chant with no translation or transliteration, unable to sing along.

I can remember being so tired at 4.00 in the morning, that on a couple of occasions, I fell into the bushes on the side of the path on the way to meditation. Thank goodness that was solved. I got in the cook's favor. At 2.30 in the morning he would make himself a strong cup of coffee, sweetened with dark Indian sugar. It was worth getting up two hours early for a caffeine reaming that brought me through the morning.

After chanting we were off into the delightful and rustic gardens of the ashram to tend plants or to clean. Then before lunch, there was a half hour chant of the familiar '*Om Namah Shivaya*', meaning 'I bow to *Shiva*'; *Shiva* being one of a thousand names for God. It is a sonorous and beautiful tune that induced a pleasing calm. Then lunch. I called it Hindu army chow and loved every mouthful. I remember I was responsible for laying down the plates. There were forty of them, thirty seven Indians and three westerners. Lunch consisted of rice, chapattis, and two vegetable dishes. Simple. Perhaps ten years of boarding school allowed me to be pleasurably uncomplaining about what an average westerner may not enjoy. After lunch most people took a nap. Then we worked for another two hours followed by forty-five minutes of meditation before dinner. Following this there was another ninety minute Hindu hymn before retiring at nine.

By the end of my five-and-a-half-month stay I was heavily burdened by what I interpreted as an 'old-fashioned religious thought system' into which this marvelous awakening was placed. Muktananda was a traditionalist, exceedingly canny and street-wise, but not 'modern' in his couching of spiritual concepts. I never liked his talks because he continually contradicted himself. Others loved his talks and were not at all bothered by contradiction. Despite all these anomalies he was a masterful guru and manager of people. He expressed an amazing intuition in his interaction with devotees for the exposure of those egoic tendencies that stood between them and the maturity they were seeking. Muktananda was not didactic in his teaching style. He taught mainly through stories, the establishment of disciplined routines, spiritual injunctions, personal firings, exhortations and admonitions, and through the unfathomable atmospherics and serendipity-producing-life under his direction.

Yet despite all this I remained spiritually and intellectually unsatisfied. What kept me around was the marvel of the awakening and the expectations of the fulfillment of the promise. At least I had expected some lasting interior shift. Nothing like it was forthcoming.

As extraordinary as Muktananda was, it was plain that he didn't measure up to the stature of omnipotence, omniscience and omnipresence touted to be the measure of the guru, according to the scripture of the Guru Gita (from the *Skanda Puranas*) and the doctrines of Siddha Yoga. These parts of the teaching I thought fatuous.

Unlike most others, as I discerned his humanness, he went up in my estimation. Other devotees who were more wedded to identifying with an idealistic belief system, became seriously destabilized with every observation or revelation regarding the true humanness of Muktananda.

Nevertheless I was willing to concede that looking at the Siddha Yoga phenomenon from another perspective, even from the highest perspective, there seemed an excellence to it. It was worthy of being given the benefit of the doubt. Unlike many other devotees, I was unable to throw my commonsense faculties into the Ganges. Feeling with my own heart and thinking with my own mind was always a tricky thing for me to abandon. For those who could, peace was less elusive. So that was the cross I had to bear in a system that didn't pay high regard to thinking.

Rather it was the way of the heart. It was the way of devotional faith wherein observable anomalies are easily overlooked.

The fruit of devotion and faith in this system seemed to me unimpressive and highly solipsistic. And to a large degree I was not moved to emulate those who found it easy to believe right down to the minutiae of the guru's teaching.

Yet years later I grew to love many of the disciplines, the order, and to love the practice of chanting. They had benefits. Simply, a well-ordered and disciplined life, particularly one including the practice of meditation and the vitalizing psycho-acoustic effects of chanting on the body-mind led to a level of general buoyancy and wellness. It was attractive, but no substantive change was forthcoming. Though what I was seeking was yet unrealized, what I was still being led to believe remained promising.

Early in my stay I was privileged to be invited to accompany Baba (a title of affection for Muktananda) in his car on a three day *yatra* (spiritual pilgrimage) to the holy sites of Maharashtra state. This was the familiar territory of Baba's years of spiritual practice.

We set out in his Mercedes, his driver on my right, Professor Jain (his Indian translator) on my left.

Baba had the whole back seat to himself. There was not much talking as we went. From time to time Baba would hand us milk-sweets and Jain and I would exchange an odd muted word.

It was at some point on this journey that Baba pressed me on the shoulder and told me that he would come to Australia at least three times. That was interesting, since Baba had never left India and I immediately thought in a very human sense how interesting the modern West might be to him, leaving the relative backwardness of his nation. Later it became clear to me that Baba had me in mind as a host in Australia.

At one particular stop, we were served a sumptuous meal, a far cry from the simple Indian fare of the ashram. I over-indulged. The next day while on our way to the *Samadhi* Shrine (tomb) of Jnaneshwar Maharaj, I started to feel unwelcome gastronomic rumblings. I casually mentioned to Professor Jain that perhaps I needed to go to the toilet. He said, 'You'll be right. We'll be there in a couple of hours.' Mind you this was the guru's chariot and no mere mortal could be seen, at least in the Professor's eyes, to interrupt the flow. Well I had my own flow in mind. I had to announce my need in another twenty minutes. The Professor was unimpressed. Things were getting serious. My stomach continued to growl angrily as I held on. I knew the situation was hopeless. I simply had to declare my need emphatically. The Professor summoned up the courage to turn around and tell Baba that perhaps I had an unmet need. We needed to stop. Concerned and embarrassed, I was amazed when Baba brushed off the whole thing without batting an eye. He had as much said, stop and do what you have to do. This was typical of the dramas created around the guru. He was far more down-to-earth and natural than people would want to ascribe to him.

So I bounded into the nearest paddy field and experienced cosmic relief. As I sat there, there followed in my mind, an interesting pun on the Sanskrit word *sat-chit-ananda*, denoting the highest bliss/reality. The last three syllables, 'ananda', of that word mean 'bliss'.

Finally we reached Jnaneshwar's tomb. He had been a remarkable Maharashtra yogic saint, who at the age of fifteen translated the *Bhagavad-Gita* from Sanskrit into the vernacular. Strangely around the same time in Europe the Bible was being translated from Latin into the vernacular. Such was his yogic prowess, that at the age of twenty-one, in front of thousands of devotees, he met his end by stepping into his own tomb to be sealed off alive.

Muktananda identified with and loved the many saints of history from this particular region of India and had been personally influenced by some of the contemporary ones.

When we arrived, it seemed to me that we had been surprised. It must have been a religious holiday, because there were hundreds of people lined up to pay their respects to the dead master. Some distance from the shrine Muktananda stepped out of the car, quickly assessed the situation, and did a full prostration in the dust by the side of the road towards Jnaneshwar's tomb, silk robes and all. I was moved. It was clear Muktananda never expected anyone to pay him deference or devotion beyond what he himself had shown to his own guru or to others he held in high regard.

On we went to Sai Baba of Shirdi's *samadhi* shrine. He was another famous spiritual luminary who died in 1918. (The current Sathya Sai Baba claims to be his reincarnation.) Sai Baba of Shirdi was a miracle worker and both the Hindus and Muslims claimed him as their own. By being his devotee or merely being in his presence, one's life became blessed and wishes were often fulfilled.

Sai Baba is like a modern day St. Christopher for Indians. Today, many Mumbai (Bombay) taxi drivers have his image affixed to the dashboards of their cars.

As a footnote, I'd say that it's hard to know how many of the claims for Indian spiritual masters are true in their detail. I noticed that in India prevarication and exaggeration were the order of the day and it seemed the culture did not have the exacting fidelity to truth that western cultures display.

Having reached the shrine, the vibrations were beautiful. Baba, the Professor and I were immediately escorted to the front of the temple, right to the foot of the saint's statue. The room was full of incense. Cymbals were being played. It was the evening worship of this statue, done with the waving of lights and chanting. This was the feeling of mystic India at its best. Muktananda's ashram had the same feeling.

We then drove to the village Yeola where Baba had spent years of spiritual practice after meeting his guru. As we drove into its center he was recognized and people came scurrying from every corner. Within a few minutes, by the well, he was surrounded by fifty to sixty people. I stepped off to the side delighting in the affection and kind regard they had for Muktananda. Here he was well-known.

On part of this journey we stopped for tea at the place of a fellow Bhagawan Nityananda devotee. Muktananda and he had been guru-brothers. It was interesting to watch them sit down on the step and 'have a good chat'. This casual style was uncharacteristic of the relationship he had with anyone back at the ashram. The trip ended for the night at the home of a well-to-do family. Baba had come to bless a business or a marriage. I cannot remember which.

To have had such an intimate time with Muktananda was unusual. At the time I might not have known the privilege of being on this trip. But knowing that he was to be the founder of a new spiritual world movement, that was here to stay, I now realize its historic significance.

One day an interesting American turned up at the ashram. His name was Franklin Jones. It was his second visit. Muktananda had spotted him as spiritually gifted. He, like me, had experienced an intense form of the awakening and was an ardent quester for the highest reality. Unlike some who seemed enamoured of the yogic life style, solace or merely something or someone to believe in, Franklin was a breath of fresh air. Here was someone who enjoyed the awakening yet had a world view or framework of thinking that was more modern and Western. Here there could be meaningful dialogue or friendly reflection on the whys, wherefores and wonders of it all.

Siddha Yoga is actually anti-intellectual as is the *Bhakti* tradition of Indian spirituality. Exceptions were found, but reflecting upon or questioning some of the presuppositions of Siddha Yoga was 'forbidden'. Franklin and I walked to the Ganeshpuri village each day, chatting as we went. I saw in him, at least at the time, a combination of spiritual awakening, discernment and brightness of mind. We had a stimulating connection. He wrote me a number of letters after he returned to America. I subsequently found myself hawking the manuscript of his autobiography – *The Knee of Listening* – around London looking for a publisher. He was later to become the famous Da Free John, then Da Love Ananda, the Heart Master, who claims to be 'the one who is to come'. He currently refers to himself as The Divine World – Teacher Ruchira Avatar Adi Da Samraj. He has changed his name many times. The story of Franklin Jones, as I'll call him, returns later.

As part of the practice of Siddha Yoga a *mantra* is used. The *mantra* is a Sanskrit sound symbol or word that one repeats. It is supposed to be imbued with the power of the guru. The *mantra* I was given by Muktananda was So'ham. This literally means 'He I am' or 'God I am'. It amounts to equating oneself with God in essence.

Inexplicably during this period at Ganeshpuri, the more I repeated the *mantra*, the more dense and heavy I became. J. Krishnamurti, a world-renowned iconoclastic Indian luminary who had influenced me before my coming to India, would have readily attributed dullness to *mantra* repetition. One day Muktananda psychically picking up my concern, drew me off to one side, and said to me through a translator, 'this type of meditation does not make your mind dull; Arjuna (the hero in the *Bhagavad Gita*) fought a battle in meditation.' I was tickled by the way he picked that up. But in general I was becoming progressively more heavily-laden by my determination to apply all that was being asked of me in this path, including bringing *mantra* repetition to the point of *ajapa japa* – that is, to the point of automatic repetition.

I'd spotted a book in the ashram library by Murdo Macdonald Bayne. A sentence I read in that book catapulted me instantly out of the heaviness I was experiencing. That sentence read something to this effect, 'How do you know that everything you have been told is not untrue?' Temporarily released from the pressure of believing anything I was deeply relieved by this question. For three days I shone, feeling lighter than the breeze itself.

On another occasion, shortly after Muktananda re-turned from writing his autobiography, (*The Play of Consciousness*) he drew me aside and talked to me for half an hour. This conversation occurred right after an explosive meditation session I had experi-enced. Much of what he said has slipped my mind by now. But he did me tell that, in this life I would achieve high spiritual heights. He also gave me tips on how to derive the best from this awakening set forth within me.

Over the next five-and-a-half-months, seven or eight more westerners came and went. Among them was an American mayor and an American LSD guru.

Encounters with Muktananda often brought paranormal experience. For example, I remember one day simply walking up to say something to his personal attendant, standing inches behind Muktananda. I suddenly had the experience of being drenched by a bucket of peace so strong as to almost take my breath away. There have been endless accounts akin to this, wide and varied, that could fill volumes. In general, Muktananda's presence radiated a force-field. It must have been a 'material' phenomenon of sorts. It was palpable from ten feet away, and was attributable to the full flowering of the *shakti* energy in him. Siddha Yoga is surely one of the Eastern religion's versions of charismatic spirituality, characterized by dynamic spiritual experiences – phenomena.

By the end of the fourth month in Ganeshpuri I was becoming restless and dissatisfied. I was inclined to take my awakening and run. I wasn't given to excesses of devotion as others so easily were. This made it much easier for them to stay and remain agog at every word and action of the guru. In the Hindu tradition the guru is the center of all sacredness, the philosopher's stone, the one through whom spiritual realization is assured. He is to be obeyed without question. His word is holy writ. The entire understanding of the guru and his role and spiritual munificence is fully described in the *Guru-Gita*. This is the *Song of the Guru,* which comes from the Indian scripture the *Skanda-Puranas*. The *Guru-Gita* had almost been lost in India. As the story goes, Muktananda heard someone chanting it in the temple next to the ashram. This was probably around 1969. Muktananda asked, 'What's that?' Sometime thereafter a heavily edited-down version, with a much reduced number of verses, became the principal Siddha Yogic scripture that now thousands of people chant daily throughout the world. When I was first there, we certainly had no knowledge of the existence of the *Guru-Gita*.

So here I was still restless and waiting for the time when it was appropriate for me to leave. Such was the authority of the guru that one didn't leave off one's own bat so to speak. I was waiting for the word.

In the meantime, there was another significant experience that became meaningful many years later. I was drinking so much chai, which is a boiled up pre-sweetened Indian tea, that it was giving me palpitations. The chai had to go. It was a hard decision because I enjoyed it so. I slipped across the road to the shop for my last ceremonial cup. Having finished it, I knew that it had to be my last. The decision had to be made. At the point of making that decision, the process in consciousness was caught as if in slow motion. It was the most executive action my mind had ever taken. Tea was gone. Never did the temptation to sip it again arise. To this day, thirty years later, not a fluid ounce of black tea has passed my lips. From that moment I knew about the power of decision. I could decide and it would be so. That was simple. It was to be seventeen years later, that at the request of a top personal development guru, I fleshed up the course called *The Decision Principle Training*®. It was designed to set up people for success, using the first principles of existence, decision. That first experience with decision was revelation. To this day I have not seen any reference to another having noticed the actual mechanism involved in the making of a decision.

One day Baba Muktananda created the opening for my departure, by asking the question, 'Have you thought what you might do?' I left for Australia expecting that I might soon get involved with organizing his first international visit in that country.

3

MUKTANANDA'S WESTERN THRUST

I was the only devotee to receive Muktananda at Sydney airport in November 1970 at the beginning of his first world tour. I was accompanied by my Uncle Edmund, a medical doctor. We were planning to use his 1932 Rolls Royce to drive Baba from the airport. Alas, it was teeming with rain that night and the driver's side windscreen wiper had packed up. I had to resort to inglamorous taxis. Seven people were in Baba's entourage, and among them was the famous Baba Ram Dass (Richard Alpert) who had been a Harvard professor, expelled for experimenting with the psychedelic drug LSD. Muktananda appeared first out of the gate and I greeted him with an awkward hug. Hugs were not usually done.

Everything around Baba had always worked like clockwork. His organization to this day is a professional and well-oiled machine. This is the legacy of Muktananda, a man of tremendous discipline, order and excellence. What followed was anything but that. There I was confronted by a mountain of luggage so huge, that it would have been enough for a football team. Keeping Baba waiting, I had to scramble for six taxis, two for the people and four for the luggage.

We finally made it to the motel around midnight. This was a transit stop on the way to Melbourne as no flights from Singapore that day could make the appropriate connection. I still remember the image of walking past Baba's room. He was sitting on the bed eating yogurt and watching television. I wondered if this was the first time he had ever seen TV.

Next day there was a big reception at Melbourne airport. By this time there were three other devotees, and their helpful parents. We had organized the whole tour together. There was a press conference at the airport. The two major Melbourne newspapers wrote stories on Baba, and both journalists, Maureen Gilchrist and John Larkin much to their amazement received the *shaktipat* awakening with all the strange attendant spiritual experiences. Today I believe one of them is still around in Siddha Yoga.

It was about a three week stay in Melbourne. We had hired a spacious home for Baba, with a large sitting room and separate quarters for his comfort. I shared a room in the same house with Ram Dass. Each day at the crack of dawn people would turn up for meditation. It was all free of charge and many would receive *shaktipat*, the spontaneous awakening. On some occasions the meditation room would be like a mad house, people bouncing around the floors, utterances coming from their mouths, speaking in tongues, dramatic breathing rhythms, rolling, shuddering, shaking. You name it, it was alive with energy. Hypnosis or hysteria were not involved (as many detractors who had not experienced it would love to believe). It was phenomena to behold. Needless to say many people were fascinated. And many came back for more, but not merely for the experiences but to be with the God-man, to acquaint themselves with his teaching, and to assess whether or not it was what they were looking for.

We arranged for Swami Muktananda to speak at Melbourne University. There were about two hundred people in the auditorium. As I drove Baba there, minutes before walking into the auditorium, he sprang it on me to give a talk on my personal experiences of Siddha Yoga. To be given zero notice was disconcerting. But a school boy public speaking practice plus the good graces of providence had it work well. The evening was well received. Both Baba and Ram Dass spoke and many with their curiosity piqued came back next day to the house for more. Baba would spend time with people in the early morning and late afternoon.

Baba asked me to run his meditation center in Melbourne after his departure. This put me into a quandary because I had become even more maladapted to the framework of thinking into which this divine awakening had been placed – that is, the particulars of the doctrine of Siddha Yoga. I'm not

67

saying that I thought the doctrine was wrong, but it fit my temperament as well as a square peg fits in a round hole.

I had to summon up the courage to confess to Baba that I just couldn't see my way clear to do what he had asked. I remember going into his bedroom to tell him what I had to tell him. He was sitting on the edge of the bed and as I moved to sit at his feet, this powerful force-field encircled me as if to hold my brain in a clamp. My thoughts seemed muscularly contained. It was an interesting experience and not atypical of the things that went on. I told Baba what I had to tell him, he said 'Don't worry. Start up a center somewhere some day.' The job later fell to a woman by the name of Pat Stewart who met Baba on this tour. I was always fond of Pat. She was a devoted exemplar of the teachings of Siddha Yoga being classically conformed to the mould of the devotee. Years later she was exceptionally kind and giving to my mother.

On one occasion I'd been experiencing automatic writing and showed some of it to Baba as a sample. It was in an undecipherable script but one that contained repeated forms. Baba gazed at it for a stretched-out minute. Then he said to me three things. 'You'll receive mantras in meditation. You'll discover the cure to all diseases and you'll receive the name of a fruit'. That last one has me puzzled.

But interestingly enough, the first certainly mani-
fested and I have an unusual gift of making accurate
observations, drawing sound conclusions and discovering remedies for my own ills and those of
others. My performance, however, is not perfect –
yet. Ho hum.

After lunch on one occasion I can remember Ram
Dass and I were taking a nap. There was a knock on
the door and Baba came in with a translator telling
Ram Dass that the police were at the door wanting
to speak to him. Ram Dass momentarily had an
amazed look on his face, because he was famous for
being one of the pioneers of psychedelic research
with LSD. 'The cops are after me,' he probably
thought. This was what Muktananda hoped he
would think. Just before Ram Dass got to the door,
Baba began to rock with laughter. It was all a joke.
It was marvelous to enjoy the deified and idealized
Baba displaying such a down-to-earth sense of humor.

From Melbourne Muktananda traveled on to America where he began to enjoy spiritual fame and
fortune.

For the next four years I continued my spiritual
peregrinations. Siddha Yoga and the awakening
were still at center stage as my primary practice and
hope.

I returned to India at least a couple of times in those years and to Ganeshpuri for several weeks at a time. I saw the miracle-working Guru, Sathya Sai Baba, at a big event in Bombay. There must have been ten thousand people present. He was lithesome and moved like a black panther. He was different. Instead of sitting on the throne prepared for him he reclined lengthwise along the front edge of the stage, tapping his hand on his thigh in rhythm to the chanting. He said very little. Chanting the divine name took center stage. As he left through the crowd he kept manifesting the grey ash they call *vibhuti*, from the tips of his fingers, the mini-miracle he was famous for.

By now tomes have been written on the man by devotees and detractors. He has by far the largest following of any God-man in India and claims to be the reincarnation of Sai Baba of Shirdi who died in 1918. Sathya Sai Baba declares himself to be the great world teacher or *Avatar* who comes to redeem all mankind.

Back in 1969 during my stay in Ganeshpuri, Larry Stroup, one of the original Americans upon my first arrival, had agonized over who was his guru. He'd gone back and forth from Muktananda's ashram to Sathya Sai Baba's ashram a couple of times. According to Larry there were ten or twelve devotees at Sathya Sai Baba's ashram when he visited. These days there are several thousand western devotees sitting in his ashram seeking his divine company – such is the increase of his popularity. Larry solved his conflict by settling for Muktananda as guru.

By 1975 Muktananda and Sathya Sai Baba met. Muktananda took exception to Sathya Sai Baba's claim that he was the *avatar* of the age, the great world teacher, none other than God Himself in human flesh. Muktananda liked to emphasize that all people were God within. 'Honor yourself, worship yourself, meditate on yourself. God dwells within you as you', Muktananda would always say. This didn't fit with the aggrandized status Sathya Sai Baba had given himself exclusively. Now I'm not sure of the accuracy of the following account, but as I heard it, they had a strained encounter. When Muktananda and Sathya Sai Baba met, my guru grabbed Sai Baba and tried to lift him off the ground. According to the scriptures, the *Avatar*, or God's incarnation as world teacher, cannot be lifted off the ground. If Muktananda could jack him up it amounted to confirmation of Sathya Sai Baba not being who he claimed to be. Sathya Sai Baba ducked, but at least Muktananda held him by the shoulders and sang a *bhajan* (a devotional song) to him about a god who fell in love with himself such that he fell from grace. If the details of the account are true, that's consistent with the sort of thing Swami Muktananda may have done. Muktananda

71

was real and fearless. Rarely would you find someone like him. Of Muktananda, Sathya Sai Baba
would say, 'Mere aspirant, mere aspirant' as a
derogatory remark, compared to himself, being God
incarnate.

This was a meeting of the Titans. By any standard,
neither of the men was ordinary. Tal Brooke, in his
masterfully written book *Avatar of Night*, gives an
enlightening account of his years as one of Sathya
Sai Baba's key devotees. The interactive dynamic of
the Guru-disciple relationship within each camp was
identical with only some particulars being different.

In 1971 during a three month stay in Bombay, a
good friend of mine, Ravi Arapurakal, a refined and
highly intelligent Indian introduced me to Acharya
Rajneesh, later to become the infamous Osho. Rajneesh lived in a high-rise Bombay apartment. He
was a spiritual teacher who had formerly taught
philosophy in a tertiary setting. He had a formidable
intellect and now had turned his hand to becoming a
guru. He taught an eclectic form of spirituality unfet-
tered by traditional convention.

It seemed to me that he was the opposite of Muktananda. Muktananda was traditional, an advocate of
discipline and order and of social propriety, and yet
was utterly spontaneous. Rajneesh, though he
preached spontaneity, appeared utterly unsponta-

neous. When asked a question, he would close his eyes and the great data-base of his mind would begin to whirr. When I lived with him in his apartment for ten days, the walls were lined with books. He read eleven of them a day. All were marked. He pored over the widest range of spirituality and every fashion of psychology and 'New Age' philosophy. At the time I was living in his apartment he was deeply interested in the fifteen books that had just arrived on Scientology.

Daily, ten or fifteen of us were invited into his bedroom. One of us would ask a question. There would be a meditative pause and the next one and a half hours would be devoted to answering the one question. I usually liked what he said. On one occasion I sat in front of him holding his hand. How different he was from Muktananda. He seemed no blast furnace. No one seemed to be home. Perhaps the Buddhists would read good indicators into that, denying the existence of self-identity as they do.

Acharya Rajneesh was to hold a meditation retreat at Mount Abu some distance from Mumbai. A friend of mine, by the name of Christine Wolf, accompanied me to the retreat. She didn't have a strong interest in any of these things. Yet in the early hours of one morning, while we aspirants were doing Rajneesh's meditation in an open field, she was up on a hillock, looking down with puzzlement and reserve. It only took one beckoning finger from Rajneesh for her to go down to speak to him. He whispered something in her ear. Within three days she was in love. What had hitherto seemed to be a pretty-well-grounded English girl, became within seventy-two hours, an ecstatic blown-out, entranced devotee. She later became the renowned Ma Yoga Vivek who committed suicide twenty odd years later, three months before Rajneesh died. She had been his devoted personal assistant and lover for many years. Rajneesh of course metamorphosed into the famous Bhagwan Shree Rajneesh, finally known as Osho. He was later noted for his having ninety-three new Rolls Royce automobiles and for starting the Orange People movement with their huge ashram commune in Oregon, USA.

It was during this retreat that I became dreadfully ill with hepatitis. I must say that Bhagwan Shree Rajneesh showed me great kindness by inviting me to stay in his apartment during my time of recovery. It was during this time that he wanted me to become one of his neo-sannyasis (disciples). He wrote me a lovely letter to this effect, which I have to this day. Still considering Muktananda my primary guru I was not willing to jump ship.

One day during my stay in his apartment a beautiful French model came to meet him. Within a day he had persuaded her to become a *neo-sannyasi*, which means one of his disciples marked by the wearing of a necklace (a *mala*) containing his picture and wearing orange clothing. There we were sitting in his bedroom at the moment of her induction. She was led in stark naked with five or six people accompanying her, while Rajneesh garlanded her with a *mala* and said a few kind words. She'd taken the plunge, so why hadn't I, went up the cry. And as a not-so-funny joke, they chased me around the bedroom trying to get me to relent in my decision. Needless to say within forty-eight hours she wasn't to be seen for dust. Rajneesh often had a yet more fleshly way with women. It was indeed so. *Some* women didn't like it as I knew from personal female friends who had encountered him in this context. Rajneesh went on to be one of the most controversial and influential gurus of the twentieth century. Again, Muktananda was utterly traditional. This man was the opposite.

During the same time in 1971 I met a most interesting man. His name was U. G. Krishnamurti. He was an iconoclast; a breaker of all images. All spiritual things were debunked by him. Perhaps he spoke with some authority since in his earlier years, according to his autobiography, *The Mystique of Enlightenment*, he experienced many of the high spiritual states of yogic *samadhi*. Many years later, after a period of down and out despair, he had an extraordinary experience that ended in the dissolution of self. Along with Bernadette Roberts, the Catholic mystic, myself, and others I'd known, the 'no-self experience' was familiar. This is a story for later.

I can remember everything about the encounter with U.G. I ascended the steps of a bungalow on Colaba Causeway in Mumbai. As I walked into a room a man was sitting on the couch reading a newspaper. 'I've come to see U. G. Krishnamurti,' I said. The man simply tapped his hand on the top of the couch, as if to say 'Sit here'. Within ten minutes, there were five of us in the room. The newspaper reader turned out to be U. G. The others were early day starry-eyed yogic practitioners. And the dialogue began.

One of them exclaimed, 'But you were once a practitioner of yoga.' U. G. replied, 'Yes, that was when I was young and stupid.' Then another of them piped up about J. Krishnamurti of international fame. And the questioner started talking about the relationship between the observer and the observed, citing a tree as the example of the observed. U. G. was getting progressively more frustrated and blurted out, 'I couldn't give a tinker's damn about that man! Never mind the tree being beautiful.' Then he gave an example of his travelling through the Swiss Alps by train. A travelling companion had gasped at the beauty of the Alps. U. G. described how he brushed this off, and said he was getting as much delight from watching a luggage tag bobbing back and forth on a suitcase. Then the subject of gurus came up.

This was a pet hate of U. G's. He exclaimed, 'These people will kill you!' It's amazing that thirty years later I can remember each of those lines. It was tough stuff. And it was certainly on the curriculum for serious-minded aspirants. His damning of every-thing cherished had a way of undoing the hearer. Some years later I shared the U.G. 'heresy' with one or two thinking-type devotees in the Ganeshpuri ashram. They loved it, in a mischievous sort of way. It was not the sort of book you want to bandy around in Siddha Yoga. One of the more senior people in Siddha Yoga loved the book.

U. G. was outrageous. He was a good tonic when things were being taken too seriously. Even the famous Ramana Maharshi, one of India's most revered 20th century saints, didn't escape his dis-dain. The two had met.

U.G. had been a confidant and admirer of the famous J. Krishnamurti for seven years, until U.G. decided and declared one day that J. Krishnamurti hadn't a cracker to offer. U.G. left his company, never to return.

I met U. G. when he was in his forties. Strangely, I inquired for fifteen years after that time among fellow spiritual travelers who had 'been around' if they'd heard of U. G. Krishnamurti. No one ever had. It seemed to me that he emerged again, at least to my notice in the 1980s, when I spotted a copy of his first book in a Bombay bookstore.

U.G. Krishnamurti's scorned friend, the famous J. Krishnamurti, once had a powerful influence on my thinking. I read him voraciously in my late teens before meeting Muktananda. The plausibility and logic of his teaching was compelling. After reading him it was very hard for me to embrace traditional values. He was the man picked and cultivated by Charles Leadbeater and the theosophists as the promised world teacher Maitreya in the 1920s. He dramatically denounced that role and dissolved the huge organization designed to proclaim him. He spent the rest of his life as an iconoclastic spiritual teacher espousing the value of choiceless awareness as the only means of realizing 'truth'.

I noticed over the years that those people who bought into J. Krishnamurti's perspective were caught up in a pride of intellectual enlightenment, a sort of precious 'I'm above it' or 'one-and-a-half-smart discerners' of all truth. I believe Krishnamurti's influence was, by and large, destructive. On one visit to India I attended a number of his lectures in New Delhi. I can remember his pointing down to the front row, and saying, 'Here sitting in front of me I can recognize at least six faces who have been listening to me for forty years. They've understood nothing.' I never met a Krishnamurti devotee who was an exception to this rule. Yet I always thought his 'technique' warranted use and his well-reasoned point of view worth considering.

Whilst on the subject of teachers who use thinking as the primary teaching mode; Wei Wu Wei had a great influence on me. Few people knew that the author, Wei Wu Wei, was none other than a six foot seven Englishman who loved horseracing. Never had I found such a clever use of words, able to take one to the brink of silence. As no one else could, he was able to 'prove' the non-existence of self and the veracity of 'predestination', or better put, present ordination. Decades later I smiled when I was exposed to the Christian doctrine of election and predestination. This was a doubly different way of coming around to a similar conclusion. The book *All Else is Bondage* is among Wei Wu Wei's published works.

Some time after Baba's first visit to Melbourne in 1970 I met Rudi (Swami Rudrananda) in Ganeshpuri. Rudi was a wealthy Jewish New York oriental antique dealer, who had been one of the early western procurers of fine Eastern art treasures. On one such visit he met Bhagawan Nityananda, Muktananda's guru. He was one of the rare westerners to have done so. This probably made him the earliest western devotee of Siddha Yoga. Bhagawan Nityananda died in 1961. The problem was that Rudi was a teacher in his own right and I don't think this sat well with Muktananda. There always seemed to be a game going on between them; Muktananda seeking to cut Rudi back to size. At this time Rudi invited me to stay with him in New York city. A short time later I flew there, living and practising with Rudi among a handful of his other students.

Properly seen, Rudi's way was very different from that of Muktananda's. He transmitted energy, felt and physically demonstrated. Unlike the *shaktipat* awakening of Muktananda, this transmission caused random joltings and twitchings and required management and development through the mindful use of pranayamic technique (breath control). This difference that I described between the two phenomena was lost to most of the people I mentioned it to, but was borne out dramatically by demonstration weeks later. Danny, one of his devotees, curious to be clearer about the difference was sitting on the end of my bed at the time. At that moment I gave over in the characteristic way, and as Danny described it, a bolt of energy left my stomach and penetrated his body. From that moment he began to have outrageous *kriyas*, the name given in Siddha Yoga to the activity of this divine energy. He went into the full gamut of spontaneous experiences – breathing rhythms, Hatha Yogic postures, cross-legged hopping and classical dancing rhythms, utterances, to mention but some of them.

At least one person after this was convinced there was a gulf of difference between the energy phenomena peculiar to Siddha Yoga and the transmission of Rudi. It was like the difference between someone tapping into and managing the energy of an 'epileptic fit' and the action of someone on the high bar in gymnastics. One seemed like an erratic surge, the other the execution of an intelligent force.

Since these times I have managed to experience and discern a number of different 'rays' of energetic phenomena. To the credit of Rudi's style, on one occasion after strenuously applying his technique during our encounters, a revolving sphere of energy the size of a tennis ball arose and began spinning in my solar plexus. It continued for several days. During that time I had a physical vitality second to none. It passed. Rudi was a tough disciplinarian. A good trainer of flaccid souls. It was the sort of strong medicine that 'New Age' people today may not be up for.

It was during these wintery months of 1971/72 on Manhattan Island that I was involved in a remarkable project. Danny, the chap mentioned earlier, and I, in the middle of Times Square, painted the external pylon structure of a multi-storey skyscraper in various colors. It was an environmental design project, designed to make the structure pretty before the sides went up. We knelt there with the temperature below freezing, rollers in hand, sluicing multi-colored paint across the floor line and the uprights of the concrete structure. Every five minutes we had to return to warm ourselves in front of a forty-four gallon drum blazing with building refuse as we'd whirl our arms round and round to get the blood back into our frozen fingers, and go on with the job. The project was written up in the *New York Times* along with pictures. This was great fun for a young man, especially at six dollars and ten cents US per hour, which was to me an unheard of rate of pay in those days.

My intention had always been to spend about four months with Rudi and then drive across country to be with the remarkable Franklin Jones, both of whom I'd met in Ganeshpuri earlier. Franklin had just set up shop as guru in Melrose Avenue, Los Angeles. As it turned out Rudi was not so thrilled about his ex-devotee Franklin, starting up on his own.

In 1973, Rudi, disaffected with Muktananda, left his discipleship. Shortly thereafter, Rudi was killed in a light aircraft crash.

I had got to know and like Franklin during our encounters in Ganeshpuri. We had corresponded and after getting to Los Angeles and spending more time

with him, I was able to experience first-hand his
personal prescription for enlightenment. The *shaktipat* phenomenon was there. The Guru-disciple relationship was there. Franklin had however created
radical departures from the traditional Indian position as regards its thought system, its motivations
and methodologies.

Franklin was impressive in every way. He was right
there with you, unlike Muktananda who was posi-
tionally aloof. His approach was life affirmative and
had nothing of the ascetic overtones of Siddha
Yoga, though indeed discipline and application of
understanding were rigorously enforced. Franklin
was a full-bodied charismatic spiritual force. He was
a religious genius with an enormous data base of
knowledge filtered through a brilliant intellect. He
had a huge sense of humor.

There was only one way in which he could not hold
a candle to Muktananda. He was not fearless. Unlike
Franklin, not once in thirteen years had I seen Muktananda fazed by anything. Since Franklin was claim-
ing to be the next thing to being the world teacher of
the age (*Avatar*) I thought that the degrees of dis-
concertion he demonstrated in many situations were
not consistent with the status he claimed for himself.
One day he refused to come out to be with his
devotees (*Satsang*) until one particular chap, who
was forceful and claimed to be able to control the

weather, was removed from the hall. Muktananda on the other hand was intimidated by no-one and nothing.

This ill-fitting trait in Franklin bothered me, and until it was resolved I was not able to bring myself into full surrender. Remember that obedience and surrender is always required of the disciples of any Siddha guru. I spent several months in his company practicing his way. Finally, my question was resolved. With thirty others I was invited to his birthday party. During the event he gave a slide show of his life. There, leaping out of so many of the slides, was this young man who simply had to be 'the big man'. I saw that his need to be the greatest of all gurus, nothing less than God-incarnate, the great world teacher, was the ultimate manifestation of the need to be adulated. Today I find his claim to pre-eminence amongst spiritual teachers to be a trifle megalomaniacal. I must however acknowledge Franklin's genius and the part he played in my education. I left his company, still retaining Muktananda's Siddha Yoga as my core practice.

In October 1982 Muktananda died of a heart attack in his Indian ashram. I had been with him twelve weeks before his death. Thousands of devotees poured in from around the world to mourn his passing. It was a huge affair.

A couple of years after Baba's death, while sitting in meditation I received a worded message from Muktananda for Franklin Jones, (currently called Ruchira Avatar Adi Da Samraj). It read like this, 'Get down off your high horse. Stop brow-beating your disciples. Make yourself unreservedly available to the general public. Do our work.' It took me sixteen years to get that message to Franklin Jones via Byron Katie, another emerging American spiritual luminary that I'd gotten to personally know and like. Had Franklin taken Muktananda's advice, I reckon he'd be pretty unstoppable. I barely met a person who could challenge him in debate, such was his command, language and intellect.

On paper at least, I think he's met his match in Bernadette Roberts, a great Roman Catholic mystic, for whom I have the dearest respect and who challenged his 'seven stage paradigm which he had accepted as the ultimate degree of truth a human being could realize'. Bernadette Roberts' realization fell outside Free John's frame of reference. Nevertheless with Free John's head to toe intelligence and formidable presence he could have made massive inroads into the spiritual marketplace. Instead he became quite eccentric in demeanor and appearance, isolating himself on his own Fijian island while lamenting that he had so few committed followers.

It would appear that he is bothered by not having

received the mantle of legitimacy from Muktananda by the declared bestowal of Siddhahood (Guruhood). By tradition the mantle of guru can only be legitimately claimed if it has been bestowed upon you by your own guru. As a demonstration of this concern, many years later in Muktananda's ashram in South Fallsburg U.S.A., Franklin sent a delegation of two of his devotees to Baba, requesting a meeting with all sorts of attendant conditions. He was to be received in the appropriate manner and given respect as to his status. Of course this was all alien to Muktananda's way. A fascinating behind-the-scenes play arose between the two. Few knew what was going on.

Each evening, during the program in front of a thousand people, Muktananda responded to Franklin's request in different ways. Franklin's two acolytes would dash out after the program and phone Franklin to give him progress reports. As I recall, Muktananda cited the story of when he went to visit Anandamayi Ma, a famous female yogini saint of India. Muktananda turned up unannounced at her house. At the time Anandamayi was drying her hair, she called Muktananda in and he sat on the floor. There were no great announcements, no delegations, no special deference or conditions required. This is how he taught people lessons about their silliness. All the while the audience were probably wondering what the context and significance of this

story was. He also relayed the image of an unperturbed elephant strolling along with a dog yapping at
its feet, all this being meant for Franklin's ears.
Muktananda was good at the full frontal as well as
the oblique teaching. Needless to say, Baba rarely
gave Franklin even a thought. Franklin's terms were
not met. The meeting between them never took
place.

Siddha Yoga under Baba, despite the marvels and
wonders associated with the awakening, was not
satisfying to my soul. Truth remained elusive and the
promises of Siddha Yoga unrealized. To date I'd
seen no-one among the devotees whose development was impressive. Yet the divine awakening
precipitated by Baba remained the core of my hope
and spiritual practice. I began to cast around for
supplementary means that might at last make the
difference.

While with Rudi in New York City along with a
number of his students, I did the Silva Mind Control
course (June, 1972). This was a four-day program
designed to induce deep relaxation and low brain-
wave frequency entrainment. It was in this state
one's preferred reality could be affirmed, healing
could take place, and windows to psychic capacity
opened. That was interesting enough. By the end of
four days' intense exposure to these techniques,
almost everyone had a small glimpse of one or other

of the promises, which predictably closed off within hours through lack of on-going rigorous application.

This is so much the case with many trainings that are based on partly-accurate observations. Consistent discipline and application are required to access some benefits. Few are capable of it. Few are willing. I was sorry that I had no companion who wanted to join me in an on-going disciplined exploration of this system. I wasn't up to it alone. It was only some years later that I would have described myself as having a capacity for the disciplined application of anything I had decided upon. This quality enabled me to trial a number of systems of spirituality with degrees of rigor later on.

4
BUSINESS, READING & PRACTICE

Providence had it that I was one of the early-birds at the doorsteps of some who were bound to become influential spiritual teachers in the West. A disciplined practice continued. I still placed the highest stock in the spontaneous gift of this intelligent force awakened in India. Amidst all this I took a job in business throughout the mid-1970s working for a small company started by an old Geelong Grammar School friend of mine. I'd loved cars and this company produced a product that made them go faster, quieter and more economically. This sounds like what I was looking for in spirituality. This was a kind time to me, until I got sick of it. I made some money, invested in the company and remain a director on the board.

Since India I'd loved motorcycles and now upgraded to a wonderful Ducati. With an old school friend I imported a Dino-Ferrari sportscar from England. On the way back from Adelaide to Melbourne, I managed to get it up to one hundred and fifty five miles per hour. Having settled back to ninety miles per hour, three Kawasaki 900 motorcyclists howled past me, riders stretched out along their tanks. Deciding to give them a thrill I jammed the Ferrari back into a second gear – I was still in third at one hundred twenty five miles per hour, with two more gears to go. Needless to say I passed them in a blink. Half an hour later they caught up with me and gave me a Von Richthofen salute as we entered the next town. A bit of fun.

During one holiday period in the mid-70s I returned to India for several weeks in Ganeshpuri. During this stay a woman turned up at the ashram displaying miraculous powers, called siddhis. She was manifesting red kum-kum from her hands and skin. Kum-kum is the powder that Indian women mix up to make a red dot between their eyebrows. People were intrigued. She remained there for a few days. She would meet Muktananda in the courtyard with all of us around. I remember Baba pointing to her and saying, 'This is your miracle, but this one is mine', as he pointed to an eight year old who was swaying in meditation.

Gurus of Muktananda's order were disapproving of the display of miraculous powers. This is perhaps another reason why he looked askance at Sathya Sai Baba, who is famous for displaying them. They were okay only if they came at the behest of the will of God – unpremeditated. According to Muktananda, getting involved in the cultivation of miraculous powers by yogis was considered a distraction from the primary goal of God-realization. Baba was very courteous with this woman and indulged her. One day during the standing evening chant, I walked to the back row and there sitting on the floor with newspapers spread out beneath her hands, was this woman, swaying. I watched with riveted attention as little stalactites of kum-kum appeared on the tips of her fingers and fell in a heap on the paper. It was no fake. I've come to know first-hand that India is the land of signs and wonders. The Biblical accounts of Jesus' miracles are easy for Indians to believe in.

It was during this period of my working in business, that Muktananda came to Melbourne in 1974 for the second time. On this occasion I did none of the organizing and enjoyed turning up most evenings as a participant to meditate and be with Baba. My confidence in the verities of Siddha Yoga was somewhat thin at this time. That awakening still had me gripped however. It never failed to express itself powerfully within me the moment I gave over to it. The physical movements, utterances, speaking in tongues, lights, raptures and revelations, etc. went on ad nauseam.

During the years of working in business, during the mid-70s, I continued with my spiritual practice and experience. On one occasion I wrote:

'As a young man I had been fascinated by the prospects of astral travel. I had read several books on it and I tried it on several occasions, but failed. So

I gave it up. I quietly put my aspirations for that aside. One afternoon, I was lying on my bed, and suddenly was aware of Muktananda appearing about six or seven feet above me, lying horizontal and looking down. Suddenly I went into a quiet state in which I became aware of my body doing extraordinary *kriyas* (spontaneous physical movements), all around the room. My physical body was inert on the bed, but I was conscious of some part of me doing all these things around the room. This went on for about five minutes. Then all of a sudden, a tunnel of energy came down from Baba upon me, and I was invited 'out', so to speak. The next thing I knew I was rising up in a blind swoon. The first thing that came to my mind was, 'I'm not going to blow it this time'. Once before I had fallen out of my body. I had lost my cool and it was all over, but this time I was not going to blow it. I remained quiet and still and just went with it, and surrendered. And I found myself over Sydney Harbor Bridge six hundred miles away. It was a late winter's afternoon and the lights in the city were starting to come on. I can remember seeing the cranes by the bridge on the construction sites and all other things. Immediately I started to experiment with this new found ability. Books I had read had stated that to go from one point to another took absolutely no time, but I found that it did take time for me to go from one side of the bridge to one mile on the other side. I was puzzled. I had an analytical approach even during this experience! I played around like this for five or ten minutes until I found myself in my aunt's bedroom back in Melbourne. She's an old woman, in her seventies. She had just gone to bed and on her dressing table were her false teeth and a pair of glasses. I was amazed that I could actually move her glasses a little. This whole adventure was getting more and more exciting. Then I became aware of discomfort in my body and I was having trouble breathing. All of a sudden I snapped back into my body. The experience was over.'

Since the beginning days in Siddha Yoga I had combined spiritual practice with devotional service and reading. By now I had collected a library of over one thousand books. There were the works of Muktananda; there were all the basic texts that described the presuppositions of India's philosophies including Buddhism, *Vedanta* and *Kashmir Shaivism* (Muktananda's favorite). J. Krishnamurti had been of influence, Alan Watts, and Wei Wu Wei. I was also intrigued by the works of Franklin Merrell-Wolff, a westerner who for a short time had been a Professor of Mathematics at Stanford University. He was initiated in a dream by Shankaracharya, the eighth century Indian master. Wolff wrote with substance and rational clarity on his experiences. He died an uncomfortable death in California around 1982.

There were a number of books on the subject of Subud that interested me from an early age. I had found them in my father's library. I took the Subud initiation in the mid-1970s, since I'd heard the manifestations were almost identical to Muktananda's *shaktipat*. Muktananda mentioned the founder of Subud's name, Pak Subuh, from time to time. It was true – almost the identical energetic phenomena set into a different framework of thinking. The approach of Pak Subuh, an Indonesian Muslim, was brought forth into the West in the early 1950s. In this tradition the awakening itself and the spontaneous process that ensued, called the latihan, was given over to tri-weekly by the devotees. The awakening alone was to be absolutely sufficient without the addition of doctrine. Uncluttered thus, it was attractive. Besides in Subud they hadn't put the lid on the overt manifestations as they had begun to do by the early seventies in Siddha Yoga. I enjoyed the latihan and the fellowship for some time but then left, because I'd had this process going in me long before any contact with Subud. Nothing had been added.

As my library expanded I became aware of the significant difference between works springing from the five great spiritual traditions: Hinduism, Buddhism, Judaism, Christianity and Islam; and the contemporary cocktail of convenient selections called the 'New Age' movement.

There are many dichotomies within the Hindu um-. brella of spirituality. A big one is that between *Bhakti* and *Jnana Yoga*. The former is the way to God through devotion, the latter the way of knowledge. The former leans towards the personal aspect of Godhead, the latter the impersonal – And I had always had trouble with the word 'God'. It had seemed too anthropomorphic to me. So in these days I more identified with the notion of the impersonal Absolute as being the most fitting pointer to the Highest Reality. Besides I had the experience of being 'annihilated' in that non-personal Absolute as a young man before first going to India. This episode is recounted later.

Though I was always capable of warmth and affection as a human being, I was not given to the emotional excesses displayed by some of Muktananda's devotees. Siddha Yoga was heavily weighted to *Bhakti*. *Jnana* was exemplified by people like Bombay's Vedantic guru Nisagadatta Maharaj, a simple cigarette vendor with a scintillating intellect and high attainment. I loved his perspectives and precepts. His well known publication was entitled – *I am that*. This conflict with devotional excesses and the absence of the discriminative common-sense faculty was a dissonant chord between me and the mindset of so many ardent devotees of Siddha Yoga. Perhaps that was my loss. Oh how lovely it would have been to be a blind believer.

Sometimes I genuinely coveted the simplicity of that gushing mentality.

In the earliest times my mind was stimulated by Buddhist writings and doctrine. Later I found that the Westerner who dons the Buddhist mindset in whatever form tends to become a trifle precious and anally retained. A Hindu high colonic irrigation of devotional chanting is usually the remedy. Zen Buddhism somehow was an exception. I was inspired by the historical Zen master Dogen, who began the Soto sect. The subtlety of his meditation method appealed to me.

Having had a light Christian enculturation in my early years, the Catholic mystics intrigued me. I loved the works of St John of the Cross, St Teresa of Avila, Meister Eckart, Miguel De Molinas. *The Way of A Pilgrim* by an unknown author thrilled me, along with *Abandonment to Divine Providence* by Jean-Pierre de Caussade. *The Cloud of Unknowing* won my attention, and there were probably a number of other Christian works I have now forgotten.

Further to all this input was a friendship with the now well-renowned Israel Regardie. He had been a personal friend of my father's. Regardie had written many books, lived in Los Angeles and was the modern exemplar of Western esoteric occultism. He was also a Reichian Vegeto Therapist practising a form of therapy that elicited emotional responses through breaking down body armor. Francis (as he was known to his friends) and I got on very well. Dad and I would see him when we were in Los Angeles. They had the discussion of Freudian and Jungian psychoanalysis in common and a mutual interest in mysticism. Regardie was refreshingly down to earth, a well-balanced man in the Western tradition. He would brook no silliness. He was intrigued by my accounts of time with Muktananda and the extraordinary awakening I had, but hated Muktananda's autobiography, *The Play of Consciousness.*

A feature of the power of my awakening was that it jumped across to others. From mid-1969 Muktananda would suggest that new devotees should come and sit with me in meditation. He suggested it especially to those who didn't seem to be having any experiences. It became very clear that this transmission could be given to others either by accident or deliberately. I was among the handful of people around the world that years later Muktananda asked to 'give the touch' during Siddha Yoga meditation intensives. Funny. The night before I was asked to give the touch in this formal way I had a vivid dream. In the dream I had walked up the aisle toward Muktananda and bowed down before his throne in the usual way. All of a sudden there was an explosion of energy in my hands as Muktananda stood on each of them. He and I walked down the aisle together and he held out a glass of water towards me. As I reached for it he withdrew it and poured it over his own head. Then he told me to go and have a shower as if to baptize/anoint myself as he had demonstrated. I had no idea what the exploding hands meant at the time. The next morning it became clear. I was asked to give the touch in the Siddha Yoga intensive weekends, designed to bring about the awakening. People certainly received *shaktipat* through this touch or by just being in its vicinity

Regardie had requested that I spend time with him, so that he too could enjoy the initiation. About all that happened to him was that he became intensely hot on each occasion. That was not an uncommon manifestation.

Regardie was the author of many books, particularly the grand definitive work on practical magic *The Golden Dawn*. Poor chap – one alchemical brew he had been working on for four years had just been chucked down the drain inadvertently by his house-keeper. He was laughing and crying at the same time, as he related the story to us over dinner.

I told him about my time and friendship with Franklin Jones. We organized a dinner. Franklin and his wife Nina came over to dine with me and Re-gardie. That was the beginning of an exceedingly short fascination Regardie had with Franklin. It ended after the first visit Regardie had to Franklin's *satsang* evening, as he was asphyxiated by the incense. Regardie suffered from emphysema.

A fruit of this short flirtation between Regardie and Franklin, was Regardie's endorsement that appeared on the jacket of the back of Franklin's first book *The Knee of Listening*. It read:

'A great teacher with a dynamic ability to awaken in his listeners something of the Divine Reality in which he is grounded, with which he is identified and which in fact he is.' *Israel Regardie*

Shortly after, Regardie's high regard for Franklin took a dive.

It was years later that Regardie became the best-known figure in Western occult spiritual circles. He died on March 10, 1985.

During these years I encountered another spiritual luminary in England. In 1971 I had the privilege of staying at the home of Douglas Harding in Ipswich. He became renowned for his book *On Having No Head*. He was a charming English architect who during a walk through the Himalayas experienced a radical dissolution of the sense of self, which left him with no reference point from which to see out. He devised a series of simple strategies for people to demonstrate for themselves that the notion of self was an assumption only and could not be apperceived by any means. He was, along with U.G. and Bernadette Roberts, another no-selfer albeit with a difference. Each of these three had a very different spin on the no-self ball.

About twenty-three years later in Melbourne I dined with Harding then in his late eighties while he was on one of his teaching tours. Many die-hard Buddhists were maddened by his insistence that the non-existence of self (a central doctrine of Buddhism) was patent and clear and didn't require any more than a few directed moments to apperceive, rather than years of diligent meditative practice. He was a man of integrity and discernment, and obviously radically 'renewed' in his own peculiar way. But he was, in my opinion, quite incapable of duplicating the substance of his knowingness in another by whatever means. To this day I own a hand-made book of his called *Testing the Incredible Hypothesis* consisting of physical devices and exercises designed to precipitate the awareness of which he spoke.

Around all these times four years of business experience continued as I persisted with my spiritual practice interspersed with exploring various other means of spiritual growth.

Among these was the experience of past life regressions. The religious theory of past lives had never been interesting to me. Thought through, it seemed implausible in the extreme. Though believed in Siddha Yoga, it was never emphasized. However, the primary purpose of this excursion was to be free of unwanted attitudes or feelings, which according to the theory, had their origins deep in the past, most likely in other lives. I had about thirty hours of this non-hypnotic processing. In response to questions asked, hundreds of images did appear, most of which could have been attributed to mere fantasy. Some few however were compelling enough to get my attention. There was an incident pictured of being trampled to death by a formation of Roman troops on the run. Feelings and flinchings accompanied the mental image. There were a number of other images that were peculiarly vivid. It was enough for me to think 'maybe this stuff is true'. However, profound doubt still lurked. There being lots of Julius Caesars and Mary Magdalenes around, along with my own experience and those of another discerning friend who had once been a facilitator of this process, I finally concluded that the whole notion of past lives was a fanciful delusion; but an understandable one. Certainly it has been shown by soft or hard research, I don't know which, that deep within the memory bank are images not attributable to this life time. The best explanation for this phenomenon, I believe, is that imbedded in the DNA of every human being is a comprehensive record of the experiences along the genetic line right back to the first humans. By a miracle of consciousness this genetically stored memory can be accessed and decoded to appear sensibly to the human mind under certain conditions. This is historical body lineage, containing all stored sense impressions and has nothing whatsoever to do with the person or spirit who believes they were *that* person in another life. Those lives were not mine at all. Metempsychosis or reincarnation was not a fact. This is about as close as I could get to an explanation without being irresponsibly dismissive.

5
A LEAP INTO
FULL SERVICE

By now I was ready to leave my job in Melbourne and swing into a full-time relationship with Siddha Yoga again. This was rather a decision taken by default. I was yet to have really found my way. After all these years, there was still no-one and nothing in whom I could really place my faith. There were many grand spiritual experiences, well-developed and compelling spiritual thought systems and some clever techniques. Quietly hoping against hope, I thought a further penetration into what I had already discovered and valued might bear fruit. In a very ordinary sense I was still someone who had not found what I wanted to do in this life. In the meantime I was satisfied with a quest for truth. I was about to launch back into Siddha Yoga with more verve.

I left Melbourne, Australia to be in the New York City Siddha Yoga ashram. A few months before, I had done a quick reconnaissance flight to up-state New York to be with Muktananda and assess whether or not I ought to re-engage myself full time. During one crowded evening program, Baba looked at me and the words were placed into my mind, 'I might have something for you to do'. This had acted as a spur to my quitting operations in Australia and taking up with Baba again. Besides I was ready for a change and the business I'd been carrying on in Melbourne had become tedious and uninteresting.

This was 1977 and my year in the New York City ashram was an exceptional one. We were all crack yogic troops. The ashram was run with energetic discipline and faithfulness. These, it seemed to me, were the peak years for discipline and application in Siddha Yoga history. Everyone had to be up for meditation in the early morning, like it or not. The ashram participants enthusiastically partook of the full daily schedule of meditation, chanting and devotional service, whether within the walls of the ashram or outside, attending to the practical maintenance of ashram business. It was a no-slouch year and I think that those of us who took part in it looked back with remembrances of 'accomplished athletes'.

It was at the ashram that year that I fell in love and got married.

In early 1978 my wife and I were in New Delhi with Muktananda. It was during that stay that I took a side trip south with a couple of other devotees to meet the famous female yogini saint Anandamayi Ma mentioned earlier. I was surprised to see that her personal attendant was a young Indian engineer named Markund. He'd been living in the Ganeshpuri ashram in 1969. His conflict had been that despite his devotion to Muktananda he was not having any spiritual experiences. Perhaps he'd found his home with Anandamayi Ma. We stayed for the afternoon. As famous and esteemed as she was, my encounter with Anandamayi Ma made no significant impression on me.

By the second half of 1978 I found myself back in Melbourne as a manager of the ashram. Baba was in Melbourne now for the third time. I can remember as he strode in toward the hall for the evening program he stopped in front of me, and with a gesture for asking 'Well?' He was referring to whether or not my son had been born. I said, 'Yes Baba, and it's a boy'. He was delighted, as he'd always said to my wife, 'Give Baba a good boy'. He walked on a few paces and as someone was stooping to remove his shoes before he entered the hall, Baba raised his arm in a triumphal gesture and said, 'Yogi Raj!' This was the moment of his giving my son his name, which means in Sanskrit, King of Yoga – Yoga, being the concept of union with God or yogic practice.

Baba always had a special fondness for Yogiraj, paying him a lot of attention. Yogiraj was a vital, alive and beautiful child. He is well-remembered and regarded by many devotees to this day.

My family continued on in Melbourne with my managing the ashram. The era of rigor continued.

Muktananda always taught the merits of a disciplined life. I rather liked that style of things. I was aware of the fruits of discipline from my years at the elite Geelong Grammar School, especially when pushing myself to the physical limits at the renowned year at Timbertop. At the age of fifteen we all had to run a twenty-two mile marathon through the undulating hills of the region. Long mountain hikes were a feature of that year. I can remember hiking through the mountains, snow falling, until my legs gave out. This kind of thing is always more fondly remembered in hindsight. Anyway needless to say, Siddha Yoga was taught as a happy balance between disciplined self-effort and devotion, spiritual practice and grace.

Muktananda was now touring the United States again and we found ourselves doing a six-month stint on staff in Miami Beach. I was put in charge of guru's *seva*, which means service to the guru. My job was to organize and manage a large workforce of devotees who were renovating the hotel on Miami Beach for his arrival. We were all involved in maintaining the tour, the buildings and the organization of bringing Muktananda's work to the general public. Thousands came from all corners of America to meet the great guru and to receive his grace. Many were delighted, and others were unsatisfied. Muktananda's reputation in the West was peaking.

My mother visited us in Miami and took delight in

her grandson Yogiraj. About this time I had the end of my finger crushed off in an accident and it was left hanging by a thread. I had it sewn back on in hospital. Muktananda gave me the assurance, 'consider that nothing has happened'. He was right. The finger took and healed completely. There had been some doubt that it would do so. We then spent months on tour in Oakland California, and later in Los Angeles. Muktananda did a six-month stint in each of these places to make himself available to the public and further his mission.

It was in Los Angeles that many dignitaries met Baba. John Denver came to play for us in the vast tent that had been constructed at Santa Monica beach to host Baba's programs. Film stars Olivia Hussey and Marsha Mason were there, and also Raoul Julia and Buckminster Fuller. Baba had a real presence that everyone found engaging. He was to yoga as the Pope is to Catholicism, and was treated with an equal degree of awe and respect.

On October 2, 1982 back in the Melbourne ashram, a knock came on my door announcing Muktananda's death. That was a big time in Siddha Yoga with devotees mourning all around the world.

Though Muktananda appeared vital and had the skin of a young man, he had suffered from diabetes and heart disease for many years. He attributed both diseases to ingesting too much ghee; Indian clarified butter. His conditions had been well-managed by allopathic western medicine.

A few years prior to his death he'd had a heart attack when on tour in Oakland, California. People were chanting the *Guru-Gita* (The Song of the Guru) all around the world, 24 hours a day for his recovery. These times were charged with devotion and the additional vitality that springs from marathons of chanting. A large retreat had been organized for Muktananda at Humboldt State University in up-state California. There were about one thousand in attendance as Muktananda was recovering in hospital. I remember his sending a most uncharacteristic letter message to the retreat. It wasn't common for him to speak in this way but he emphasized the fact that we were already God if only we knew it, and that there was nothing to be done. *Sadhana*, (spiritual practice) was just a constructive way of filling in the gap between birth and death. This is my paraphrasing. At the end of the letter his final words stated, 'Please release me from your love.' This last sentence was edited out of the letter when it was published.

Within hours of the announcement of Baba's death, my wife was on a plane to India with my son Yogiraj. They arrived just in time to see Muk-tananda's body from afar before it was ceremonially entombed. People poured in from all over the world. Up until three months before Baba died, my wife (Godavari) and son, were with him in the ashram. I had left four months prior to this to get work in Australia to supplement our income. In addition I had been concerned that Yogiraj come back to Australia because his health was taking a beating from amoebic infection and a deficient diet.

I had noticed the effect of vegetarianism on thousands of people over many years. Some thrived on it and others' health fell apart – seriously. Refusing to acknowledge the fact that vegetarianism could be anything other than divinely ordained, I saw a number of people's health collapse, limping on in a half-life state for years. In my case I recognized what was going on early, but before waking up to it I would go to every homeopath, chiropractor, naturopath, herbalist, witch doctor under the sun. Sometimes a slight amelioration of my devitalized state would happen, but nothing significant. It was only after a huge gesture of being utterly fed up with deteriorated health that I decided to feed myself on steak. It was a dream to my system. My body screamed with delight. Within one month of my reintroducing beef as a remedial strategy and in measured doses, along with explosive exercise, I began to be renewed. It took me two years to fully regain good physical condition, and to repair the damage to a body system that was genetically unsuited to a vegetarian diet, no matter how carefully crafted. No way did I want Yogiraj to fall into this pit. So I was quietly anxious that he leave as soon as possible.

So, a lovely play occurred between my little five-year-old son, and Baba. Here I was in Australia asking my wife and son to return and there was Muktananda teasing little Yogi to stay. That was all okay by me, but I remained really concerned about my son's physical well being.

Though he never declared it, Muktananda knew he was going to die soon and he was asking people to stay. There were numerous stories to confirm his foreknowledge, over and above the usual prevarications and misreads common to the excessively devotional mindset.

Muktananda's way and behavior spanned the full spectrum of humanness, free of all pretensions and preciousness. He remains the only man whom I have looked at closely who seemed wholly free of fear. Not once did I see him fazed by anything. Never once did I see him appear self-conscious. His personage embraced both the mundane and the high ranges of spiritual mystery. The scope of his dominion was awesome. All his responses across the range seemed impeccably appropriate. Amongst the highest dignitaries he was one of them; at home with all. When my wife and son abruptly returned to India for

Baba's funeral, I had not expected to follow. But two months later I was quietly moved to down tools in Australia and return to the ashram in India.

Gurumayi and Swami Nityananda were now on Muktananda's throne. They were both the appointed successors. They were brother and sister and were children of a family of long-time devotees. From childhood they'd spent a long time with Baba, particularly on weekends. I still have a mental picture of Gurumayi as a very young teenager sitting in the courtyard with Baba.

They were in their early twenties when they received the mantle. Gurumayi was older than Nityananda. Their appointment as successors had come perhaps a year before Muktananda's death. A few thousand westerners were present in the ashram at Ganeshpuri for their investiture; a grand religious event presided over by a Hindu *Mahamandaleshwara*, a sort of loose-form cardinal. There were days of Vedic rituals, Vedic chanting, featuring Brahmin priests. It was a visual spectacle to behold and the occasion raised up high levels of energy and awe.

As a matter of fact, at the moment of their investiture we thousands witnessed a 'miracle'. Right there in the dead heat of summer, out of a cloudless sky, a heavy cloud appeared dumping buckets of rain on the event. This was more than a mere meteorological

111

aberration. Muktananda knew it. He smiled. It's always believed in India to be most auspicious for such a particular thing to happen. Similarly when I went on the private pilgrimage with Muktananda in his car described earlier, it began to sprinkle with rain out of a summer sky as we approached the village of Sai Baba of Shirdi's shrine. Baba commented, 'The Gods are welcoming us.'

Of course in this whole milieu of Indian religiosity people easily slip into hyperbole and exaggerated tales are told. But out of all of this can be drawn stories of substance and accuracy, that attest to the miraculous and the paranormal, with a consistency that demonstrates that in the world of Siddha Yoga there is a current of value and mystery, palpable and almost measurable, that defies neat categorization. Yet what fruit was it bearing for me? None.

So I was again back in India after Muktananda's death, this time with the two successors. Within a few days of my return Gurumayi and Nityananda, while sitting on their throne together, asked me if I would become a manager. I gave the reply, the tone of which was not meant to be disrespectful, but was undeferential compared to the way people normally spoke around there. I responded with the words, 'You must be joking.' I had no ambition to ascend the ranks nor did I expect to be there for very much longer. One thing led to another and six months later

I found myself as one of the ashram managers. At this time, Western Swamis (monks), from the old guard (who had taken vows of renunciation and celibacy) in Siddha Yoga, were still around trying to adjust to the new regime. They had their own problems to work out. Some bit the dust; some stayed on. The relationship between the two successors Nityananda and Gurumayi, however, was evidently strained.

Everything that happened in Siddha Yoga happened within an apparent milieu of excellence, order, discipline and fine aesthetics. The ashram was nothing less than a jeweled garden, forty or fifty magnificent acres of botanical splendor, lovely buildings, marbled courtyards, studded throughout with tall statues of Indian deities, painted up in Play-Doh colors. It was an enchanting place and was a credit to Muktananda's stewardship. The strengths of Muktananda's own character filtered down through the ranks of the whole movement, which is characterized to this day by punctuality and excellence.

Ganeshpuri ashram, like other long-standing ashrams of Siddha Yoga, was a repository of this energy called *shakti* – the energy of the awakening so often referred to. If you were at all sensitive, you could feel it in the environment. The more intense the particular *shakti* in any part of the ashram, the more it felt like pea soup without the ham. The whole place was imbued with a beautiful vibration, one that was both palpable and muscular. To sample a few minutes in Muktananda's bedroom, for example, a place where the 'epicenter' spent hours every day, was an empirically amazing experience. That vibration was definitely there beyond any imaginings. It was unlike other discernible vibrations emerging from the bodies and premises of teachers from other lineages that I had known. This whole Siddha Yoga show was far from a dry, mentalized, intellectual form of spiritual practice. It had a throb to it and issued from viscera and beyond. I was to realize many years later that ultimate truth had nothing to do with *shakti* energies or vibrations of any particular sort or nature, as delicious and tantalizing as they may have been.

We spent a stretch of eighteen months in India at this time. Four discrete camps existed under the one roof of the successors: Gurumayi's devotees, Nityananda's devotees, and those who could go either way. There were also those stuck on Muktananda who had trouble with allegiance to either successor. Somehow I found myself as a manager under Nityananda. I had no particular preferences, but that was fine since Gurumayi was a bit foreboding. They were such opposite characters. Nityananda friendly, easy going, spontaneous and likeable. Gurumayi highly responsible, set apart, orchestrated, diligent and especially caring, at least to those who were her allies. She took her role very seriously and considered herself the custodian of a treasured lineage that had implications for the world far into the future. Nityananda was all too young and fun loving. He hadn't sown his wild oats. Muktananda had dumped a suit on him that really didn't fit. I think some two years later when he was ceremonially stripped of his position and title of guru he sighed a sigh of relief. There are volumes in all of the details of the unfolding story of Siddha Yoga. I'd walked in the corridors for many years, and as an 'old timer', as the long time devotees were called, I was often able to witness things directly that many were not privy to, and at least to be told of facts that others would rarely hear.

I never had a problem with the utter humanness of Muktananda and his successors – a humanness coupled with expressions of mysticism with all attendant spiritual capacities. Indians love to pretend that their spiritual luminaries live only in the upper reaches of pure spirituality – omniscient and omnipotent – and only sully their souls with the pleasures of the world for the upliftment of their disciples and never for their own gratification. You'll see this idealism and fantasy spelled right out through their scriptural wisdom songs, like the *Guru-Gita*, the *Avadhuta Gita*, the *Ashtavakra Gita*, and *Ribhu Gita*. It's fanciful spirituality with muscle. Muktananda's favorite philosophical system, *Kashmir Shaivism*, describes the manifest world as the play of consciousness – the dance of Lord Shiva. At least to this degree playing on the field for pleasure was legitimate. As did Muktananda in the last twenty years of his life, both successors enjoyed nothing but the absolute best that money could buy. Fine. The pleasure side however, finally got the better of young Nityananda. It had become too overt. His sister became disquieted about excesses, remaining within the 'walled city' of discretion. It was all too unbecoming for a perfected being of the Siddha lineage to be gallivanting and racing about in sports cars among other things. He had to go.

The building events leading to the coup d'etat made an amazing story. It had all the elements of an intrigue held within a medieval castle. Shakespeare would have made something out of it.

In the earlier brewing times of the discord between the two successors I ended up being part of an advance party for Gurumayi for a forthcoming tour of some towns and cities of India. It was a really great experience. There were five of us in the car, our driver, an Indian Swami, a wealthy Indian industrialist, an American and myself. The idea was that we visit devotees in the towns or cities that Gurumayi was due to visit. With the industrialist on board we were taken from fine Indian home to fine Indian home; nothing but the best. In these homes I had the most delectable Indian food I have ever tasted. On one occasion the food was served on solid heavy silver plates. It was the other side of India we westerners don't usually see.

Wherever we went there was always great devotion to the guru – lively chanting, and the fervor of co-operation for the welcoming of the Great One to come. The trip was plainly enjoyable. Before we started out I was handed an envelope full of rupees – Indian money. There must have been a couple of hundred dollars' worth there. 'What was it for?' I asked. I didn't get a straight answer, but it was evidently just pocket money for my trip. I was surprised and touched. Gurumayi was being very generous. Rarely in those building days of Siddha Yoga were any resources used for anything other than the requirements of the ashram and the comfort of the guru. Everyone, including staff, had to pay their way.

At some point during the tail-end of this trip I found myself on the verandah of the Bishop's mansion in Nagpur sipping tea. This huge house had been built by the church in the nineteenth century and now belonged to a well-to-do devotee, his wife and five daughters. He had been the secretary to the Maharaja, a position of considerable status. As I sat there a telex was handed to me, instructing me to get on a plane immediately and come back to the ashram. I complied, very curious about what lay behind the request. I got back and Nityananda asked, 'Can you get your bags ready in a few hours. We're leaving for Germany.' So Nityananda, his female attendant (Devanyani) and I flew out that night, on Swissair to spend ten days as the guest of a wealthy soccer star devotee of Nityananda's. Nityananda was having his ashram quarters renovated to match or exceed the opulence of those of Gurumayi. This was to be a holiday interlude to get out of the way while the work was being done. The soccer star was a wealthy car-dealer. In his stable was an AMG Mercedes, an Audi Quattro, a 500 SEC Mercedes Coupe, and a limited edition BMW. The choice was ours.

One day we'd zoom down to Frankfurt to buy clothes. The next up to Hanover to look around. Each evening it was a different fine restaurant. It was basically food, fun and holiday. All the time Nityananda, as affable as ever, was enjoying himself. Worldly antics.

Siddha Yoga is a powerful system whose power and purposes are not merely mind-born. I think of the Shakespearean quote, 'There are more things in heaven and earth Horatio, than are dreamt of in your philosophy.' It just happened that I was exposed to all these things. Through Siddha Yoga and the providence of God I have walked on the other side of the mundane veil. Spiritual adventures, experiences, visions, cognitions, realizations/signs and wonders, had become familiar, as had the human side of an altogether different life than dreamt of by the common Westerner. I took it all as part of the divine orchestration. In my *soberest* moments I offered no judgments or condemnation on the characters involved. This was a critique. It seemed to me that everyone did their best within the limitations of their own experience, understanding and background. None could claim to be perfect, including those whose lot it was to be spiritual guides.

On another trip on our way to New Delhi there were five of us in the car. My wife, my son and an Indian were on board. An American was driving. Approaching a village, much to our dismay, we ploughed into a teenage water buffalo. The car lurched off the road and came to a grinding halt in the bull dust. I leapt out to assess the damage. We still looked drivable. I jumped back in. The car strained to limp away. Almost from nowhere people started appearing. As the accelerator was planted I looked up and there was a man about to launch a rock right through the side window. Crash. It was smashed. My wife was in the back seat huddled over our son. The next thing you know a rock smashed through the back window hitting our Indian friend on the head. We were trapped. This was serious. There must have been thirty people around the car.

The mob started manhandling our Indian friend who was bleeding from the head. The American driver stood outside the vehicle shaking – petrified. We had to do something. I yelled for someone who spoke English and tried to cool down the situation mustering all possible diplomacy. You see, their buffalo had been killed.

Much to my wife's credit, she blurted out 'Ask them what they want!'. That line did the trick As she lay huddled over our son, I negotiated recompense for the damage. What did they want? A hundred rupees – around ten dollars. We remained alive. Never have I parted with ten dollars more gladly. The crowd dispersed unhanding our Indian friend. The car limped off down the road. Two miles away it ground to a halt. We had to be towed by a tractor to the next town for repairs. We showed up at a panel beaters at 11.00 pm. All the boss's workers were asleep on stretcher beds on the street, the coolest place to be in a hot country. He stirred them into action and by seven o'clock next morning they had replaced the windows, panel-beaten the crumpled fenders and replaced the radiator. That's a part of India for you.

Our Indian friend was not having a lucky streak. Later that day when in another town he took a motorized rickshaw, which was nearly bowled over. He was on a brink again.

Four weeks later, after we had arrived in New Delhi to work on the New Delhi ashram, Indira Gandhi, India's Prime Minister, was assassinated by her own Sikh bodyguards. From the roof of our five storey ashram, we spent a week watching fires burning. Three blocks away, the home of a Sikh customs officer, was harassed by a crowd of angry Hindus. Expecting to scare the crowd away the Sikh customs officer went onto the roof of his three-storey home with his family. From there he fired a shot at the crowd. The mob stormed the house, climbed to the roof and threw the whole family to their death.

This was a small part of what happened during that week, as vengeance for the death of Indira Gandhi. But remember our Indian friend – the unlucky one? At the time he was on his way back from attending a relative's wedding in Agra, the place of Taj Mahal fame. He told me that on his train were two Sikh teenagers. As the train approached the station they saw a mob waiting on the platform. Hurriedly the passengers tried to hide the Sikh boys. They failed. The boys were dragged out onto the platform and bludgeoned to death with iron bars.

India is a land of strange contrasts. It is the cradle of ancient spirituality. You can feel it in the air. It is normally a peaceable place where everyone feels safe. But things can erupt into madness with the slightest provocation.

This all happened during a period of scrambling to get the Delhi ashram ready for use, and for the arrival of Gurumayi, whose quarters were being made palace-like. Nityananda was heading up the operation. It was around this time, especially when Gurumayi arrived, and after being garlanded by an elephant, that her disdain for her brother and his efforts was obvious. The chill in the air was palpable. She was not at all impressed with any of his preparations including her quarters. Of course there was far more behind all this than just the physical accoutrements. She turned and left within an hour.

On one side trip from Delhi with Nityananda to the Mahamandalweshwar's ashram in Hardwar, we were bathing in the upper reaches of the Ganges that pass through his ashram when my wife and I had a moment of sheer horror. We looked around and our five-year-old son Yogiraj was nowhere to be seen. For an instant we assumed the worst. He'd been carried away. Moments later, to our relief, he showed up safe and sound. Gulp.

One night I remember sitting around a roaring fire in front of the Delhi ashram fuelled by the building site debris. We were tired after a hard day's work. It was announced by Nityananda, who'd risen late, that we were going to make a dash through the night to a holy spot on the Ganges River near Hardwar. Sometimes I found it tedious trying to keep up with our twenty-two year old successor. We jumped in the cars, three of us in convoy and bleary-eyed we began picking our way through the mountainous roads of the Himalaya regions at high speed. Three times that night I nearly ran off the road. Only coffee saved my life and the lives of my companions.

There were many shenanigans like this. It was sometimes fun. The spirit was always congenial. Nityananda was likeable and indeed we chanted and we meditated also. But I still craved substance and became weary of mucking about in this fashion.

To its credit Siddha Yoga in general was life affirmative. There was always a good admixture of celebration, work, spiritual practices, and there were enough serendipitous and synchronous happenings to ensure against living a plumb ordinary life bereft of the influence of the spirit. What it all adds up to I'll never know. The promises were far short of being met. But for those who were unduly fascinated by spiritual experiences (that by now I was sick of) and for those for whom it was enough to have someone or something to believe in, this life-style was fine. How long could I keep things up? At this point there was nothing more interesting to do. Baba originally talked of three, six, nine or twelve years to reach Self-Realization. As the decades passed he jacked it up as far as eighteen years, and then before he died it had stretched to three life times. He was adroit at window-dressing. Maybe Machiavelli, the fifteenth century Italian statesman was right about all fools having to be lied to for their own good. I was not pining in a silly way for the climactic experience of Self-Realization. Signs of substantive change of heart and mind, of renewal, of sanctity and of a genuine love, peace and a coming to rest in the truth, is what I would have settled for.

I saw no sign of this in anyone, and I had a quarter of a century to track it. Surely with time alone, people matured. Surely under discipline and rigor people were strengthened. Time matures. But the product of Siddha Yoga was no more impressive than that growth that might have been acquired by any old meat-and-potatoes man with a modicum of common sense. I never could see the connection between flailing-armed spiritual emotionalism, and the calling forth of character that perhaps marked some of the Christian saints I had read about, and whose conscience had come alive in Christ. Nor could I equate flashy spiritual experiences with headway and truth. It seemed to me that those Siddha Yogis with a rich interior life, and those that were flushed with devotion for the guru, were just as likely to be dissolute and morally moribund as they were to be anything else. Perhaps this was a rank form of spiritual materialism in the sense that phenomena and paraphernalia were the attractors and measures of substance. This form of mysticism was starting to look like a false standard of spirituality. I'm not saying that true value and substance was not somewhat recognizable to the gurus, but not even they could deliver on the promise. People just loved that jazz.

Not long after this Indian trip, I found myself at the South Fallsburg ashram again in America. There was a changing of the guard. A friend of mine took my place as Nityananda's key man. I had been delighted to receive a phone call from Australia beckoning me to a corporate consulting contract down there. I was off like a shot. Until the call came I had stayed within the ashram situation until something showed up that really interested me. As part of my scanning for supplementary means over these years I had learned a lot about personal development strategies, including communications skills, belief engineering, negotiation skills, etc. A capable Siddha Yogi friend of mine, through sheer *chutzpah*, had won a huge corporate cultural change contract with Telecom Australia. He had only one other man on his team at this time.

He pulled me in to build up the ranks and work together to develop a series of programs, both personal and organizational, to re-engineer the corporate culture of Telecom Australia. The company was to be set up for success in an emerging competitive market place. A short time later he hired a couple of ex-Siddha Yoga western swamis. With this team we got the ball rolling, designing and delivering a highly professional corporate cultural change program, utilizing the practical end of personal and organizational development. It was pragmatic, free of all vestiges of mysticism. I believe that the *Vision 2000* project, as it was called, was finally one of the world's largest corporate cultural change programs ever undertaken. Some say it was one of the best.

Those few years spanning the mid-80s were kind to me. I enjoyed doing presentations. This constituted the peak of my professional working life. However the gloss began to fade when I was offered a contract half the duration I had expected. This gave me an opportunity to bow out. It was not long after this time that I became a much-pained marital statistic.

So often I saw the black and white syndrome of thinking among those who passed through spiritual pathways. The tendency was always to throw the baby out with the bathwater. What they were championing one moment they were vilifying the next. I sought to find value wherever it could be found and give it respectful acknowledgment. Discovering *what worked* was my serious concern.

By now I'd weaved my way back and forth between the continents of Australia, India, U.S.A. and U.K. And an aggregate of over four years were spent in India. Siddha Yoga, with its gurus, as my core practice and allegiance to date, along with those others with whom I had a serious brush, were all contributors to a data base of experience which further honed my discernment in a reach for the ineffable. I never slammed the door on anything. Nor could I wholly embrace it as long as there remained significant anomalies that indicated the presence of 'iron pyrites' or fool's gold. And in my reflections I tried not to bring judgment on mere trivialities.

By now I'd had a rigorous dose of Indian mysticism, taught on the practical end of personal and organizational development and explored the better 'mind dynamic' programs of the 'New Age' movement.

6
THE DECISION PRINCIPLE

Having left corporate consulting I felt free and independent. I had a chance to strike out and share those things that I had found of value with members of the general public.

In the past I'd explored a number of popular, high-end personal development courses. Noteworthy among them EST/Forum (now called Landmark Education) This course was a sort of mind-power secular boot camp. It was a rigorous call to thinking and getting your life straight, taking a stand for what you believed, being responsible, committing and being clinically efficient in all areas of life, sticking to agreements, being punctual etc. Over a million people have done this course since the 1970s. Its founder, Werner Erhardt, was Muktananda's American host in 1971.

There was a similar genre of successful courses around at that time. A Canadian, John Kehoe, had come out to Australia running a course called *Mind Powers*. He was getting two thousand people a week to introductory programs, spending a fortune on advertising, and signing up a couple of hundred people at two hundred and fifty dollars each. It was a model that worked well. A friend and student of Kehoe's, Kerry Riley, took up where Kehoe left off. They probably struck up some franchise agreement, as Riley continued to teach his course and run the model with considerable success. My mother had always followed me into everything I did and it was for her benefit that I made the suggestion that she attend. I had not done the *Mind Powers* course. However in India, sometime earlier, over a prolonged period I carefully experimented with its materials and principles. After this carefully conducted trial I found that affirmations and creative visualizations simply do not work, except for the odd moment of serendipity. But Mum always seemed to be keen and was at her best when surrounded by buoyancy and positivism of the 'mind powers' culture. She was looking for a way of enjoying better health. *Mind Powers* suited her. She claimed a health improvement and she would happily give an articulate testimony to the same in front of Riley's one thousand patrons. She ended up doing radio ads for him.

I got to know Kerry Riley through this. A point came where he needed a new program to deliver. I never found out the real story behind this, but I guess his contract for using Kehoe's materials was running out. Being aware of my background, he asked me if I would create a new course for him. I accepted the challenge, not having a clue what I might put together. So I went over to Adelaide in South Australia and hived myself off at my friend Peter Kelly's home, with the purpose of fleshing something up. Lo and behold the experience of the executive power of decision back in a Ganeshpuri tea house sixteen years earlier became the foundation of the training I was to create. It was called *The Decision Principle Training*®, the Service Mark of which I registered in several countries of the world. It was a three-and-a-half day course that began by inviting the participants to recognize that the decisions they had made, either wittingly or unwittingly, had orchestrated their entire destiny.

I came up with a way of helping people to be clear about what they wanted to do with their lives. They were then introduced to the actual procedure for making a conscious decision. Seven or eight core decisions were to be made, on the basis of their new clarity of direction. These decisions would continue to move them long after they were made. The course was designed to be of the essence with no fat. I'd known there was really only one decision necessary to make, a decision for capital T Truth or God. Following this decision, truly made, all of life would come into elegant correction. But that was too much for the average course aspirant to swallow. Perhaps they needed to come to that conclusion themselves, and as long as they were discovering and deciding upon the basis of their benign natural affinities, that would lead them closer to home. That's how I would have put it in those days.

I spent a week grooving Kerry Riley in on the

course. He liked it. And we thought we might do something together. Before we got to the point of making the decision to do so, it was clear that a joint venture wasn't suitable. I withdrew with my training.

Shortly afterwards I was introduced to the name of a new high-end personal development training called *Avatar*. Paul Rogers, a good friend and fellow spiritual traveler had done it. We had often swapped notes over the decades.

One of my presentations in corporate consulting was on the subject of belief engineering. It incorporated the recognition that the beliefs we hold will perfectly reflect the way we think, feel, act and behave. Rarely would we outrun our beliefs. This was not new. And I had experimented with a number of ways of re-engineering our belief sets before coming up with *The Decision Principle Training.* ®

Now Harry Palmer's *Avatar*® course came along. He'd used this sanskrit word for its name and registered it as a Service Mark. Beliefs were his theme. Beliefs determine one's experience. Change your beliefs and thereby change your life. This sounded right and was half true. His peculiar contribution was to add to this basic framework of thinking, a series of clever techniques to dissolve the mental mass attached to limiting beliefs rather than to merely manage them cognitively. Trying to talk yourself

into or out of a core belief whether rationally, or
with the use of affirmations and visualizations, was
fruitless. So I thought that Palmer's claims and signs
of peculiar inventiveness were worth a try.

Interested, I flew to Los Angeles to the home of
Marilyn Ferguson, whose work had seminal influence on the 'New Age' movement. She had written
a one million best seller book *The Aquarian Conspiracy*. There were eight or nine of us attending.
The course was two thousand dollars. It ran for
about four days. I was intrigued and surprised that
one of the two *Avatar* teachers; masters as they are
called, was Ingo Swann. I'd seen Ingo written up as
a renowned psychic. He had been a psychic research
subject with Stanford University for sixteen years
and enjoyed the highest rate of accuracy ever
recorded. He worked with the CIA developing remote viewing protocols for psychically discerning
the nature and whereabouts of certain military instal-
lations in Russia. I grew to know and like Ingo.
Later I stayed as a guest at his home on my trips to
New York. Ingo was at the *Avatar* course independently of his psychic capacities. He'd found Palmer's
work worthy of exploration for his own reasons. He
is no longer associated with Palmer's work.

I was keen to see what Palmer's approach would
yield. The four-day period was rigorous. It required
staying power to gain an experiential penetration of

the materials. By course's end I enjoyed an uncharacteristic interior relaxedness. It was as though some knots within me that I did not know existed had unraveled. On a scale of effectuality *Avatar* was looking pretty good compared with what I had experienced before. This was in 1988, the very earliest days of Palmer's work.

Four weeks later I flew to the other side of the United States to be trained with four others to deliver the *Avatar* program professionally. This training spanned ten days and cost an additional three thousand dollars US. Years earlier my cringe around the utilization of money as a means of exchange for services rendered had dissolved. Truth wherever I could find it, was my first priority. If it was going to cost serious money, so be it.

During one of the exercises I had an interesting experience. I was sitting opposite one of the trainers, exercising to lock in a desired conviction or belief. Suddenly the width of my visual perception began to increase. The trainer wanted to continue the exercise. I declined because something interesting was happening. I got up and walked out into a foyer and stood there for twenty minutes watching two men chatting. One was sitting on the ground with his back against the wall, the other was standing. They were talking in earnest. As I looked at them, the whole scene appeared as an illusion. They were no more real than puppets in a Punch-and-Judy show. As I perceived this I was fascinated. It was a full blown experience, Technicolor, cinerama, surround sound. It wasn't some mentalized thing. Life and what I was witnessing was an illusion or a false impression and not as it seemed to be. It wasn't as though common reality was worthy of derision, rather it was a muted joke. Here there was no weight to any element of it. Even as I watched I knew I was enjoying the classic Vedantic realization that all life is an illusion – a dream – a mere seeming. This is what one branch of the great Indian yogic tradition promulgated as a key truth. Here I was in the middle of it experientially. As I watched I even recalled, as people came to seek Muktananda's advice on some dire problem, he was simply unable to share their gravity about it. About the most complicated answer he could ever have was 'Just drop it'.

Seeing from this perspective nothing really mattered as I had assumed it did. This perception shut down after about twenty five minutes. It was a serious eye-opener. It was many years later, that on this point I had a clue to the basis of the whole Eastern tradition of spirituality and how it contrasted to our western one. To the Buddhists, life is suffering. To the Hindus, it is an illusion or at best a play of consciousness. Squarely faced, both these view-points are life-negative. They in no way affirm the creation as it is plainly experienced. Both viewpoints are a dodge and a highly sophisticated one at that. A whole metaphysical, philosophical edifice is built around this dodge, including a way of life, a set of values; and for those in earnest, a system of spiritual techniques.

The presupposition arising from the apperception I experienced above, arises from an understandable conclusion, but one that is flawed. The aspirant assumes that what he has experienced, because of its 'loveliness or superiority', is true reality and therefore something to be aspired to. A filter has been pulled off and a new dimension of reality experienced. The luminary then sets about saying 'Look what I have found; devote your life to its discovery'. It begins to waylay a whole culture and begins punching holes in the bottom of the bucket of plain life clear and simple. The realizer has missed the point and taken everyone else with him. All he's experienced is a window into another 'dimension' or category of existence. Big deal. I'd seen through a lot of these windows. This is not the human category of existence. To aspire to establish oneself in that and to bring everyone else along with you is, I believe, to proceed from a gravely mistaken assumption. The champion of such quests may have experienced this state for a second, a minute or a day. Through Providence's gift some can know it for maybe a week. Perhaps in the history of mankind there are those to whom it has fallen for half a lifetime. But how significant is it really? It's all an understandable error. Such experiences lead to forms of spiritual idealism. Perhaps Eastern systems of spirituality in no way conform to the real reality for which by design, we were created to enjoy. This is what I was beginning to suspect.

By the end of this course I knew that Palmer had discovered some clever tools for creating experiences and temporary forms of relief from the sharp edge of reality. There was enough left in it to warrant further attention. But by the last day of the course, a good friend Richard Redmond and I, both concluded that there was important missing data in Palmer's paradigm. I believe Palmer had not discerned the bottom line at all. Scientology and *Avatar* are kissing cousins, focussed on the ever- revolving management of change. In these thought systems there is the denial of an absolute; there was no sense of a bottom line beyond change.

I liked Harry. He probably liked me. We had some interesting conversations; in fact we struck up well enough to have a diving holiday on New Caledonia together with some other French friends. In the meantime, I'd finished the *Avatar Master Teacher Training* and returned to Australia to back off from all things, and wait and see what presented itself. Seven months later, in a most casual manner, I decided to give the teaching of *Avatar* a go. Much to my surprise, people queued up for the course. I probably had a better way of speaking about it than most *Avatar* masters who commonly struggled.

Among the technologies around, *Avatar* was certainly efficacious. It was worthy of further exploration by me as a teacher and practitioner. I ended up being one of the more successful teachers of the program around the world, delivering it in New Zealand, Australia, Singapore, Switzerland and North America.

Palmer was a good researcher with crisp insight, but I believe he lacked the intuition and blessing arising from life's foundation. His materials could only penetrate to a certain level. Besides, his clever observations and techniques were lost on useless attempts to create 'one's preferred reality', with self at the center. Rather, I believe, they were ultimately being used to reinforce the creation of one's preferred *un*reality and to further a narcissistic illusion. By observing over time those people who climbed the ladder of his promise, it was plain to see an increasing degeneration and disintegration of their lives rather than the opposite. Here insight and error have been mixed together in an attractive and heady cocktail. *Avatar*, as with all 'New Age' and personal development programs, plays on the creation of the phenomenal. They rely on the creation of effects to continually excite the interests of their patrons. Peo-

ple are endlessly fascinated by the revolving phantasmagoria of experience, secular or spiritual.

Even the Hindus knew this well. In that tradition
there is a distinction between the gods and the sages.
The sages have come to rest on the bottom line,
whereas the gods endlessly cavort through the
planes of existence enjoying endless and various
degrees of pleasurable dominion, only to find at the
end of a day or a million years it all comes to
nothing. God and His rest is yet to be realized.

Palmer's most expensive prescription is *The Wiz-
ard's Course* which costs seven thousand five hundred dollars U.S. It takes nine days. It promises the
dominions of the gods. It didn't deliver. Regrettably
the further up his course one proceeded, the less
substance was found. Any interesting contribution of
the *Avatar* materials is contained within the basic
Avatar course. My four years as an *Avatar* master
were a gracious time. It was to be one of my last
flings amongst the works of others. I'd had so many
adventures, had been exposed to so many perspectives, understandings and technologies. I had diligently trialed a number of those that in my own
estimation, distinguished themselves. A little more
was to come.

7
THE END GAME BEGINS

In the mid-1980s I was only on the outskirts of the Siddha Yoga schism. Following my departure to Australia for the corporate consulting days, I kept a thin but unbroken relationship to the body of Siddha Yoga. I maintained a healthy respect for Muktananda, Gurumayi and Nityananda. After all, the whole adventure had a seminal influence on my priorities, mindset and directions, albeit with serious reservations. There still seemed a current of powerful value in Siddha Yoga. It was appropriate for me to maintain at this time cordial relations and a favorable connection to the inner thread. I felt that had been somewhat sullied by my being around at the time of the great schism. I was intuitively pressed to fix it, so I requested permission of Gurumayi to come to Ganeshpuri with my son. I was politely invited to remain in Australia, but my son was welcome. That was evidence that some besmirching had taken place at least in their eyes. I made the request again the next year. All was well. I returned to Ganeshpuri for three or four weeks.

The schism had occurred three years earlier and I was not savagely placed onto the back foot, like so many of my old friends who remained champions of one or the other successors. It was taboo in the Gurumayi camp to mention her co-successor and brother Nityananda's name. New and middle-comers were not to be confused. And within the Nityananda camp there were always fomenting covens of conversation, antipathetic to Gurumayi. Interestingly enough Nityananda himself stayed pretty clean from this unsalutary talk. Such is life. The human condition seems a mad thing. Great gurus from whatever tradition seemed as much an expression of it, as they were embroiled in it. I sidestepped this bi-polar friction. I was casting elsewhere for my salvation. I was no longer invested as some others were.

Despite this background it was lovely to be back in Ganeshpuri. It had been a long time. The enchantment remained. Siddha Yoga was a vibrant, charismatic form of Hindu mysticism, with at least one foot on the ground. And the ashram itself was a place of beauty. I felt pleasantly neutral and appreciative. It was a bit like returning to see an old friend with whom I did not have much in common, but whose company I could appreciate for other reasons.

It was around Christmas time. I was one of the people put in charge of organizing the Christmas decorations. They'd just flown in a hundred thousand dollars worth of decorations from Singapore. These had to be set up around the huge open hall that held a couple of thousand people for the special day. The walkway approaches were lined with decorations as well. As usual, getting everything right turned out to be a mad scramble. This was usual in

Siddha Yoga, straining to the limit and to the eleventh hour, putting up with commands and counter-commands throughout the process. Yet magically – and I don't use the term lightly – final outcomes were always impeccable. The dynamics of the Siddha Yoga community served to knock the sharp edges off everyone's ego. This was typical of all Siddha Yoga projects. There always seemed to be an unseen divine hand in the whole thing with a shining final outcome.

In this case you've never seen such a sight. The place looked spectacular and it was all devoted in this Hindu ashram to celebrate the day of Christ, his birth, his teaching – Christmas Day.

Can you imagine? They'd flown in from England the Cambridge Choral Choir. There must have been twenty of them. An American violin virtuoso was flown in – a young man who ended up receiving *shaktipat* and did not know what on earth had happened to him. Among devotee performers were a master acrobat and a renowned American jazz saxophonist, named Illinois Jacquet. The day became a program of talks on Jesus Christ, the singing of Christmas carols with the Cambridge Choral Choir, impresario entertainments and delicious food. All this was set in the jeweled environs of the ashram. Of course Gurumayi gave the key address as the living spiritual Master. She remained at the center as always, as Jesus Christ, respected as another great being, was being acknowledged.

At two o'clock in the morning I bumped into a female member of the Cambridge Choral Choir. She was sitting in the garden, tears in her eyes. I inquired of her. She said that never in her life had she known such an extraordinary and moving Christmas Day. Many would have said the same. And that was Christmas in a Hindu yogic ashram, done of course, for the benefit of the one thousand plus westerners present.

Within this period, back in Australia, I had brought the *Avatar* course to the senior teachers of a growingly popular program worldwide called the Hoffman Quadrinity Process. This course was the best of what psychology had to offer. It was a professionally delivered, rolled up and packed intense eight-day residential program. It was supposed to be a final gasp, turbo-expunging every psychological aberration that was supposed to be running one. I thought I'd exhausted my interest in the psychological paradigm, but perhaps not wholly. The Hoffman teachers all loved *Avatar* and many of them subsequently became *Avatar* trainers. Some left the Quadrinity Process, and some did not. I knew and liked some of the teachers. They still held forth glowing reports of the benefits of the Hoffman Quadrinity Process. Against my better judgment I took one last drink from the psychological well.

I suppose the only worthwhile thing about this experience, was that it finished psychology for me forever. I can remember feeling turgid as I left this pillow-beating nine day catharsis. Its program is not as mad as it sounds. The psychological world view was behind it. It was professionally delivered. But the program seemed to me misleading, cementing in the doctrine that your parents (though now forgiven) were the source of your every aberration.

As I drove away from the course I implemented a clever *Avatar* technique. Within seconds I was rising up out of the turgidity like a phoenix from the ashes. 'Whoops' I thought – what was the use of just spending three thousand dollars if I didn't give the tools of this program a decent try to assess what outcome they had to offer? So I let myself descend back into the glugginess of that world view to evaluate its product over a longer period.

This was not one of the more valuable of my experiences. In fact my old friend Paul Rogers, with whom I had often swapped notes, had also done the program. He confessed years later, that up until the time that he did the Hoffman Quadrinity Process he had often experienced a spontaneous bubbling up of joy. Never once did it arise again after doing this course.

As my *Avatar* days were tapering off another opportunity arose. Mumbai during the seventies there lived an extraordinary man by the name of Nisagadatta Maharaj. I mentioned him earlier. He was a humble cigarette vendor and a great *jnani* – a knower of the highest spiritual realization through the path of knowledge. The transcription of his teaching dialogues became well known in the West. They were published under the title *I Am That*. He was a brilliantly articulate and enlightened Guru. His *Vedanta* teaching attracted me, but I had never met him. Muktananda had eventually frowned on people visiting this man, declaring 'So what if he is enlightened? Who else can he bring to enlightenment?' You see Nisagadatta was not a dispenser of the vibrant charismatic form of meditation as Muktananda was. His primary focus was the cultivation of correct understanding, discernment, and the right use of attention.

Nisagadatta was now dead and not having met a master of this genre, my curiosity remained. So in 1993 I flew to Lucknow India with a French *avatar* teacher friend, Hadrien Jousson to meet H.W.L. Poonja. *Vedanta* was one of the six schools of Indian philosophy and was one of the few teachings I had keenly wanted to investigate. But I had never found a Vedantic guru worthy of inspection. I had a two week encounter with Poonja. We had a good conversation at our meeting. He told me about his visit, many years earlier to Ganeshpuri, and his meeting with Muktananda. He acknowledged that the way of Muktananda was the spontaneous way and that it was by the touch that Muktananda's yoga was set going.

Each morning we spent a few hours with Poonja. He dialogued with person after person encouraging them with the use of the question, 'Who am I?' in order to trace back his or her attention to the source of awareness. He was a joyous and playful man, most probably the embodiment of what he taught. I gave myself carefully to the understanding required, and while jogging in the Lucknow Botanical Gardens, I slipped into the pre-verbal recognition to which he was pointing. Still it was another experience.

Before he died in 1997 Poonja spawned a whole generation of American teachers who claimed renewal and revelation through his work, conforming to the Vedantic model of truth. I encountered most of them along my way in America.

I was starting to see that not even cognitions or realizations of the highest sort had anything to do with the truth. The pattern goes like this – each cognition or realization is followed by delight and hope. One is overcome by excitement and an anticipation of stable renewal. Buoyancy generated by the experience or insight peaks, plateaus and drifts away.

It's probable that many of the western teachers in this genre, convinced of the veracity of their knowingness, continue to teach out of memory and intellect, justifying their good counsel on the basis of experiential convictions of the past. Their patronage depends somewhat on the assumption by their audience of their abiding enlightened state and the possible fulfillment of the promise they hold out to others. Experiences took place. Experiences were easy to come by. Somehow they were never 'it'. And neither were feelings. I could see that spiritual life and progress could easily be predicated on feelings or experiences. Really it was a ride on a merry-go-round forever to nowhere. Even the 'non-experience' of abiding at the root of awareness itself in the botanical gardens in Lucknow, was a cosmic conjuring. Oh how seductive it all was.

Slightly to one side of these teachers, but included in the same general category was the Australian Barry Long. I spent seventeen days on retreat with Barry. What to say, what to do? The panoply of spiritual possibilities was endless. Barry was okay. Even the cleverest or best was starting to not impress me. He propounded an understanding of how men and women could get along, he claimed to be *the* world teacher and prescribed techniques for the use of attention for spiritual breakthrough.

Back in Australia, taking stock, it was clear to me that I had explored broadly and deeply for twenty five years. So much of all this stuff was starting to look the same.

Back in the seventies *A Course In Miracles*® had briefly caught my attention. This course had been purportedly dictated by Jesus Christ piped through a professional woman named Helen Schucman in New York, who in the mid-1970s published the document. Presumably this was Jesus Christ's second comment.

Fifteen years later I read the text of *A Course In Miracles* carefully. I must admit, it proved the most well-developed, coherent argument for transcendence I'd ever found. It was a brilliantly-constructed argument. If it delivered even on a quarter of its promise it would be looking good. This was worthy of careful application.

Rather than practise and study it alone, and appreciating the synergistic value of fellowship, I mustered fifteen friends and acquaintances from the spiritual track. We agreed to meet in my home each Monday night. A friend, James Amson and I, hosted the evening. The fifteen were committed and ready to go. To excite their interest in joining the work I wrote them a letter that serves as a concise summary of *A Course in Miracles*. Excerpts from the letter are set out below.

'The *Course in Miracles* sets out to invalidate conventional human perceptions. It takes the reader down every highway and byway through which we seek satisfaction and 'proves' through rigorous logic, that none of these investments can ultimately deliver on its promise.

It replaces a common resort with a spiritual one, postulating the idea that only an identification with God can ever bring ultimate fulfillment. The basis of this argument is that human perception is a mis-take on Reality – a skewed perception. Only by establishing a true-take on Reality can we be released from the pain engendered through an identification with the false.

Life is a dream it says – an apparency – the tooth and claw of which is no more real or substantial than the images that pass across our vision at night in dreams, which, at the time, we think so real. Only upon awakening do we smile with relief. And so it is, *A Course in Miracles* claims; with our waking state, from which we can also awake when truth dawns upon us.

This notion that common perception is an apparency

only, is a tenet of the Hindu Tradition of *Vedanta* and some forms of Buddhism. It is a theme that recurs time and time again. This, or other core declarations of *A Course in Miracles*, has been reaffirmed throughout history by the experiences of mystics from the Hindu and Buddhist traditions.

The purpose of the Course is to awaken us to real Reality by first retraining the mind to think differently. It does so by creating a comprehensive and water-tight thought system to replace our current one. This system is designed to catapult us beyond itself to a direct experience of the reality to which it points.

Couched in Christian terms its usage often causes recoil amongst those unstudied in religious thought, those who have not grasped the profound inferences of religious terminology, or those who have had unfavorable associations with their Christian upbringing. With increasing discernment, however, the real meaning of these terms is revealed and old pejorative connotations fall away, leading one to the reservoir of wisdom common to so many of the scriptures of the great religious traditions.

The Course has come, it says, to redress the message of the past and to re-establish the true teaching as it was originally intended. The interest of the writer springs from an appreciation that the Course is in perfect accord with the perennial philosophy – a constantly recurring ancient theme. It adds to it a structure, logic and comprehensiveness, that enhances its application for spiritual enlightenment. Though the way or slant of the Course may not be suited to the temperament of all aspirants, this problem is more than compensated for by the compelling nature and utility of its arguments.

It is a work of beauty. And to those who have explored broadly and deeply it may come as a helpful revelation to be taken on *in toto* or as supplement to other spiritual means.

It calls us to a radical reinterpretation of our moment to moment experience of life and invites us to relinquish all responses based on fear and antipathy and to replace them with those of love and trust. This call is not extended as a mere exhortation but as a rationally developed proposition. The notions of willingness, forgiveness, love and trust in the Holy Spirit are at the fore of its appeal. These are, it says, the keys to liberation. It gives sound reasons for us to take them on as life's central theme and tutors us each day in their use.

It is through its understanding, structure and exercises, coupled with our willingness, that the *Course in Miracles* conveys us to liberation. It is one way. Consider it as you please.' And the letter ended.

Our group began with fifteen people and ended with five. That was a pretty average attrition rate. Those that left and those that stayed had diligently practised the daily exercises and communally discussed, and reflected upon, elements of the text. Daily exercises were prescribed by the text as the means of retraining the mind.

It turned out that most people found the text heavy going. I thought it was wonderful. I could barely put it down. I believe that none of the others got through the text, though they practised the daily exercises with discipline.

Over the years I had met quite a number of people who had done *A Course in Miracles* or claimed to have done it. I now had an experiential appreciation, along with my companions. What staggered me was that never once had I encountered *A Course in Miracles* student who, judging by how they talked and behaved, had ever heard of it let alone practised its principles. The disparity between its claims and its effectiveness were massive. This was evidenced within myself as well. How could I so fully appreciate the truth of something, generally and most specifically, and yet still continue to think, feel, act and behave as though I had never heard of it. For the life of me, I could never find anyone who had got the least demonstrable benefit from the Course.

This became quite a philosophical conundrum for me. Months later I sat on a verandah in New Caledonia looking out to sea wondering what was behind all that. I could see clearly that the merely cognitive approach; the type of approach of *A Course in Miracles* and many other forms of spirituality or psychology, was useless. It seemed to me that the impact for change does not begin in the mind. Nor can it be substantively influenced therefrom.

That left me with the conclusion that if any volitional means were to be employed for transformation one would have to find a way of influencing the instinctive limbic brain, directly bypassing the analytical neo-cortex. Dismayed by the ineffectiveness of the Course's propositional and logical approach, I became inclined to suspect that the thinking mind pretended to be so influential but really was just the justifying and rationalizing mechanism of a deeper imperative lodged in the individual's native disposition.

This set me really determined to break through on this one, so I launched a number of stratagems simultaneously. Some old and new elements were involved.

I had always had two forms of meditation: the spontaneous kind, begun by Muktananda, and the other rather more formal kind using a *mantra*. Of a number of formal styles that I had experimented with, I found that the superior mantric technique was that of Transcendental Meditation. This was particularly in regard to its understanding of the way to create conditions for meditation to occur easily and effortlessly. I had trialed the TM method assiduously for one year. By now I had an experiential appreciation of a range of approaches giving me solid comparative value to come up with the best. Using the skill thus acquired, I salvaged quite a number of failed meditators, and derived great satisfaction seeing them return to successful practice given the better means.

By 1994, with *Avatar* finished, I had plenty of time for personal spiritual practice. I began to up the ante, in the quest for finding what really worked – what *really* made a difference.

Disciplined application of spiritual practices was not difficult for me. I'd grown to love it. It was all part of the meaning of my life. But in all this I was able to include exacting experiments designed to produce tangible results. One among them was to find a way of redisposing my interior being from that of the common trip, of whatever form, to a sublime disposition in accordance with the highest loving spiritual principles ... and at the same time to seek to accomplish a few other constructive effects. I produced about forty hours of non-conventional guided meditation tapes, drawn from my understandings and experience. I was to use these for my own coaching and edification. I'd also experimented with low brain-wave entrainment music to place atop my formal meditation. Zygon and Master Charles' tapes were among them. Master Charles had been one of Muktananda's swamis for years. There were other brands I have now forgotten. A small sampling of them was enough to assess which suited me.

I settled on a system called *The End Program*. I took this course to the fourth level of deep brain wave entrainment. A clever argument was spun for the value of getting into states of deep rest. Here the analytical processes of thought settle down. Quiescence is achieved – deep calm. Supposedly psycho-physical regeneration is enhanced at these levels. It's basically an old Indian idea. Maharishi Mahesh Yogi of TM fame popularized it, and the sound men had added some audio technology..

Over three years I did a consistent nine hundred hour experiment with this system, as part of a broader program.

I'd get up at 4.30 am and start the day at five with two and three quarter hours of spiritual practices. Sometimes for short periods I had friends banging on my door at 5.00 am to join me.

I'd begin with one hour of silent meditation, followed by a thirty minute tape-guided exercise that involved a specialized use of attention. I would then chant the *Guru-Gita* for forty minutes, the psycho-acoustic effect of which was buoying and vitalizing. This effect was quite apart from whether you believed in the meaning of its words. I'd end the morning's practice with forty five minutes of the spontaneous *Shaktipat* meditation.

Chanting was an interesting subject. I hated it when first introduced to it in India. I thought it silly and religious; a superstitious practice. Being required to conform to the ashram routine over the years I grew to enjoy it. But I found further benefits when I disciplined myself to practise it in measured doses each day. The chants were sung in Sanskrit and this particular language is claimed to have some added value. I noticed that forty five minutes of chanting each day created an invigoration that lasted for hours. It was a great tonic.

Years later I was fascinated to discover the research of Dr Alfred M. Tomatis. He was a French Ear-Nose-and-Throat Specialist who had become the world authority on the beneficial effects of chanting and sound on the psycho-physical system. His discoveries began with measuring the vitalizing effects of chanting among the monks in a Benedictine monastery. The more they chanted, the more vitality and buoyancy they displayed. In the 1960s, the Church Council of Vatican II, the development of Pope John 23rd, watered down the monastic life and drastically reduced the number of hours chanting in the monasteries. Tomatis had been called in to find out why the monks were sitting around like limp rags, instead of displaying their characteristic energy levels typical of the monks for the last eleven hundred years. Chanting, it turned out, was the vital ingredient. From this base he discovered that there were certain tones, rhythms and inflections of music that stimulated the brain directly, independent of religious considerations or beliefs. It turned out that the ear was a channel for brain stimulation independent of its function for hearing alone, and thus further stimulated the entire nervous system. It was interesting to have corroborated these effects in my own experience.

Simultaneously I was putting together a *Complete Reality Training* pathway designed for building the momentum for transformation. It consisted of the best I had been exposed to, extrapolations therefrom, and the long years of experience and personal revelation that I had been gifted to receive.

The *Reality Training* comprised eleven pillars designed for optimum progress. (I renamed the *Shaktipat* awakening *Veritas*, to divorce it from some old confusing yogic connotations.) To give an idea of my thinking at this time, the pillars are set out below. Though it reads like an informational brochure, it does summarize what I believed I drew from a thirty-year spiritual adventure. It encapsulated what was required to excite people's interest in joining the work.

(1). *Veritas* (Latin: Truth) is a supremely beneficent awakening. This entirely spontaneous and dynamic process automatically expunges a being of all past impressions that have stultified awareness, (including the effects of aberrating personal life experiences and blocks of a cellular and genetic nature). In this way it spontaneously draws one into an experiential penetration of one's true nature opening up new levels of experience, peace, joy and spiritual union.

In contrast to *Veritas*, all man-made or mind-born prescriptions for spiritual enlightenment, no matter how sophisticated or clever, are fraught with the limitations of the ego (limited self) of which they are a product. The action of *Veritas* suffers no such limitations. The Absolute becomes one's guide and the same Supreme Intelligence that turns a seed into a flower and keeps the planets on their axes orients itself towards the spiritual unfolding of the individual.

The Veritas Seminar thoroughly explores this theme. It is designed to see that each participant experiences this specialized ray of grace – the gift of spontaneous awakening. During the seminar we are familiarized with an understanding that facilitates the full fruition in enlightenment of this spontaneous process.

(2). *The Decision Principle* addresses the bottom line in a new and unique way. It develops a compelling appreciation in each participant of how decisions wittingly or unwittingly made, have orchestrated one's entire destiny and how such a destiny can be changed by the making of new decisions. The course elicits a pristine clarity of direction. It clarifies what decisions are, *teaches the actual procedure for making them* by revealing the mental mechanism involved and shows the way of making them stick. This is the missing information. The universe is a marionette on the strings of your decisions.

(3). *The State Zero Training* brings the freedom that comes with clearing the weight and concerns of mind. The cocoon of limitations thins and dissolves, returning us to Source. We move forward into the discovery and actualization of our Essence Calling. With disappointments healed and possibilities mobilized, this can be the full turnaround. Clarity, calm, and the willing capacity to act in accordance with our best intention, is its product.

(4). *The Decision Master Training* is a Certification Program for those who would like to become licensed teachers of *The Decision Principle Training.* *The Decision Principle Training* fills a need by being pragmatic and results-oriented, with the added value of defining the realities and distinctions necessary for appreciating it as the First Principle of existence. *The Decision Master Training* is for those who would like to more deeply integrate this First Principle, to rest further in the peace of how it works and combine the qualities of vital performance coupled with ease and calm. Finer distinctions are explored and experientially penetrated. We move boldly forward toward crossing the critical mass that breaks the bonds of limited 'I'-centered consciousness.

(5). *Praxes* (Latin: The Practices)
This pillar provides an opportunity for associates who have deeply appreciated the value of our trainings to expand their integration even further through the regular daily application of the tools provided. In addition *Praxes* provides training in an effortless technique of classical meditation and instruction in two other practices from the Great Spiritual Traditions.

(6) *The Thinking Course*
Thinking, self-referral and the capacity for integrative and classical enlightenment are the features that distinguish humans from animals.

Thinking is a primary resource. It can be taught. Formal thinking tools exist and can be enjoyably applied in a structured way for all difficulty resolution and the design of a better way forward.

(7). *The Grand Enlightenment Retreat* is the gift that establishes within us the quality of steadfast application of the practices and understandings that lead to integrative and classical enlightenment. The bonds of torpor and ignorance that fix us to degrees of unsatisfactoriness are broken, creating a freedom and buoyancy that arise from understanding, discerning practice and soft-edged discipline. The fundamental practice of the spontaneous way of *Veritas*, meditation contemplation, chanting (biosonics), work and play, are all elegantly combined to build a momentum for transformation. Deep practices from the Great Traditions and contemporary revelation are utilized to make the difference.

(8). *The Veritas Community* is run on an idea being ventured. A happy fellowship based on a common set of spiritual values is a helpful element in the training for transformation in consciousness. Such a community offers opportunities for excellence in our environment, daily life and livelihood. Opportunities would be afforded for daily spiritual practice, contemplation, meditation, and also for workshops, which lead to deeper experiential penetration of the central issues of *Reality Training* and establish the habits that lead to the full flowering of spiritual and temporal life. Its way encapsulates the essence of an integrated approach to living and provides the impetus and framework required. To people whose deepest desire it is to discover what is Real and True and who wish to share it with others, and who have sufficient imagination and humor to establish friendly relations, this invitation is made.

The *Reality Training* sets out to build the momentum for transformation in consciousness and at-onement.

(9). *Learning to Meditate*
This is one of the first practices on this path. Its ease and simplicity make it a joyous part of each day. Its practise diffuses stress, and creates wellness and vitality. This meditation is a preparatory daily practice which establishes a firm foundation for a life of buoyancy and spiritual progress.

(10). *The Etruscan Program*
All of us experience degrees of wilt. Our body either serves us well or drags upon us. *The Etruscan Program* is designed to create a functional wellness and vitality that is uniformly achievable. Based on sound observations and empirical research, it sets one up with a body that becomes a vital and co-operative friend, through a carefully developed formula of exercise and dietary hints that work.

(11). *Success Education Series*
This series consisting of seven 120-minute presentations, set one week apart, explores the fundamental principles governing success in several aspects of *conventional* life.

i) *Success and how you define it.*

ii) *The Communication Training*
We live our entire life in the context of relationship. Communication is the bridge. As a key to success you will learn the fundamentals of effective communication.

iii) *Developing Rapport*
Being in rapport is creating the finest possible relationship. You will learn and apply the four factors that are inextricably linked in creating rapport and understanding.

iv) *Negotiation Skills*
Life is a negotiated pathway with friends, bosses, children, spouses etc. This presentation cultivates the ability to discover and implement win/win situations in all relationships.

v) *Possibility Thinking*
This presentation draws a distinction between two styles of thinking – problem and possibility thinking. It enables one to harness the power of constructive

thought, leading to better ways forward.

vi) *Goal Setting*
Discover the goals that will enliven and fulfil you. Clarity equals motivation and clear directions mobilize attention and energy toward fulfillment.

vii) *The Power of Belief*
Your personal beliefs are the real forces that determine your thinking, feeling, behavior and actions or lack of them. Your life will be a reflection of what you really believe. Identify what's blocking you and move on to success.

Each presentation, including prescribed homework, is designed to bring about a personal integration of the materials so that they become a part of one's standard operating procedure.

Your *Re-Source-Fullness* is proportional to your willingness to decide for it.

The foregoing was an example of the way I was thinking at the time. I was ready to go. I even registered ® some of these names as service marks.

I was enthusiastic about the power of this program and believed it would do everything I expected it to, with a lot of help from grace. That help was not forthcoming. By this point I wasn't willing to go out and whack the beast to get people's attention and patronage. The whole program had to go forward graciously or not at all.

I began teaching *The Decision Principle* and had already created *The Decision Masters Training*, which was a further step in understanding, and provided the training necessary for people to teach the basic course.

The Decision Principle training went well over a period of three years. The program cost $1,250 per person. I taught it in Canada, Singapore, Australia, New Zealand and France. It was a good course. It had unique features. I believe it was based on sound observations and an accurate conclusion. After all there was nothing in life but the consequences of our decisions whether wittingly or unwittingly made. For people to recognize this and to understand more about the way the principle worked was of value. I enjoyed the experience of teaching it.

On *The Decision Principle* course, unannounced, I would offer people the opportunity of receiving the *Veritas* Awakening (*Shaktipat*). This was the transmission I have been referring to all along and led to spontaneous spiritual experiences. Never before had I made this awakening available in a formal context. With rare exceptions everyone had a significant experience, from visions to spontaneous physical movements, to deep calm. The phenomenon never ceased to amaze me. Still after all these years it had tantalization value. I yet believed that something substantive might come from it, both in myself and in others. The experience was often delicious. It was only the fruits of significant regeneration that were absent.

So *The Decision Principle* and *Veritas* were in place. I also began teaching formal meditation, which I thoroughly enjoyed teaching and practising. Many of my students were well-to-do. Many medicos were among them. And come to think of it a disproportionate number of them were women. This reminds me that in the first fifteen years of Siddha Yoga, there was always a fifty/fifty ratio of man/ woman attendance. Today it is running seventy-five/ twenty-five in favor of women. This ratio I believe pertains to the whole 'New Age' movement today.

During this period I was quite unsure of the destiny of my life and work. I was adamant not to get cranked up into a pitch of promotional activity.

It was over this period of time that I gave a great deal of attention to my own spiritual practices. Otherwise there were long periods where nothing was happening. I enjoyed recreational rides on my Harley-Davidson motorcycle. Between 1993 and 1997 I returned to America twice and paid a couple of visits to the Nityananda Temple at Gurumayi's South Fallsburg ashram. This temple was erected in honor of Muktananda's own guru Bhagawan Nityananda who died in 1961 (not to be confused with the co-successor of Muktananda, the young Nityananda). It contained a huge one-and-a-half-times life-size statue of Bhagawan Nityananda. This small temple environ seemed to me like the energetic epicenter of Siddha Yoga worldwide. The *shakti* energy here, it seemed to me, was more powerful than that at Muktananda's *samadhi* shrine (tomb) back in India. On each visit to the temple I was shown an experience. While sitting there one day, the image of a banking airplane was slam- dunked into my mind. Under the wing were markings just as seen on Sydney's roads. They indicated that this lane is stopping; change lanes. By jove this seemed to indicate I'd be changing paths. Then two days later, as if to confirm it, quietly sitting in the same spot, again an image was presented with the same definition and intensity. This time there was water being poured from one disposable cup into another. The point here was that the living water was the essence. The particular container (path) was not significant. This was another indication that I would be changing paths, but I had no idea what it was pointing to specifically.

On the next visit I had two more experiences. In this vision there was a huge book with perhaps millions of names in it. Against each name was a comment of perhaps no more than one or two words. A page fell open and as a finger moved so did my name come into focus. Against my name were the two words 'too independent'. Surely this had been my Achilles heel for all those years in Siddha Yoga. This yoga requires of the devotee complete surrender to the guru and belief in his/her status as the binding embodiment of divinity itself. Not being able to stretch to that, I was too independent. So perhaps this experience indicated a general downfall for me, not just pertaining to Siddha Yoga. The next experience I had was a clanger. I couldn't deny its authenticity. Dropped right into the middle of my awareness were the words, 'You are on a self-created fantasy trail'. These words did not simply occur to me, as thoughts occur in the normal sense. It was not merely a striking thought amongst others or even a personal revelation from myself. The words were slam-dunked right into my mind. It referred to my independent spiritual drift and the creation of the complete reality training, in which I had placed so much stock. I conceded that the message was true and that my way indeed was folly.

But what was the alternative? There was no going back. What I had created was free of all forms of hokey religiosity and superstition. It included a palpable and dynamic 'divine' awakening, a well-developed thought system consistent with perennial

spiritual values, and powerfully functional techniques. What more could providence ask of me –
show me something better. Just show me!

The next few years were quiet. I wondered if and
when I'd find my feet. The practices continued. I
experienced two strange episodes in the next three
years. Over a few days I was brought to the recognition of a self-imperative that had been running me.
'Listen to me, I'll tell you the truth'. It was the
underpinning of a teacher identity. So as this identity
of mine slipped away to nothing, so did my interest
in being at the vanguard of any new inventive spiritual means.

A year later I experienced what I called the 'death of
ambition'. I never considered myself a particularly
ambitious person. But after this experience lasting
three or four days I would have been happy to sit in
a deck chair and look out to sea for the rest of my
life. That would have been enough. Any knot of
unrecognized drivenness that may have been within
me unraveled, leaving me in a state of peace and
freedom with nothing to accomplish. Even the quality of my sleep changed significantly.
These two experiences were more like visitations
than the product of common rumination. It seems
they were divinely ordained as part of getting me
somewhere. Where? I didn't have a clue. I knew
about the importance of surrendering to divine prov-

idence but these long periods of hiatus were stretching my limits.

It was at the age of nineteen, before I ever went to India, that I had a spiritual experience equal to the crowning glory of all – the experience of ultimate truth. I had walked onto the back verandah of my father's home and seen, through the silhouette of a tree, a seagull passing through the sky. It was a moment of beauty. What followed was beyond words and beyond even experience. There was total annihilation of self and ineffable ecstasy. The moment I realized what had happened, the experience disappeared. The experience could not co-exist with the recognition of its being had. Its most distinctive feature was the dissolution of self. Very strictly speaking what took place could not be even described as an experience. An experience consists of *someone* being able to experience *something*. No-one was left. Nor was there union or oneness, only dissolution absolute. And somehow, unalloyed ecstasy was present.

This experience was the end of the road. There was no question of beyond. The concept of beyond or more is always attendant to a notion of self. When the whole dichotomy of self and other disappears, when there exists not even the oneness or union, then nothing can be said, yet ... this was the essence of Godhead before forms and labels. This apperception was non-conceivable and remained for me the Ultimate and Absolute Reality.

I was amazed, but it left me completely puzzled as to how the Hindu luminaries could talk about *Self*-Realization as being equated with the ultimate truth. If I was to be given all the words in all the languages of the world to point to this experience, the last one that could be used would be 'self', (either with a small 's' or a large 'S'). Crossed over green eyebrows, or black dogs would be more fitting words than 'Self'. Years later I found the Sufi term *fana*, which means 'annihilation in God'. This was close but annihilation ... would have been closer since we are talking about God before 'he' is named. Now it seemed to me that the Hindu term *sat - chit - ananda*, which indicates the highest reality in that tradition, would be best translated as a double negative not-not existent, – not-not conscious, – bliss. That's about the best discursive indicator one could come up with, that vaguely tallied with my experience.

Some ten years later, when sitting at Muktananda's feet in South Fallsburg over a period of a week, I *disappeared* in this absolute sense about five times but without the attendant bliss. There was a sense of cosmic relief in the absence of self. As soon as self returns to recognize its absence, the 'experience' cannot continue.

Interestingly to me, then or now, there was no inclination at all to relate this experience intuitively or intellectually with the Buddhist concept of 'no self'.

Despite having this marvelous 'experience' I was intrigued by its having zero impact on my life. None. All that remained was having had the memory of an experiential access to the highest reality. Okay, I was grateful for that. But it did not add one jot to the quality or texture of my conventional life or spiritual activities.

Years on, I discovered a book that caught my attention. It was called *The Experience of No-Self* by a Christian mystic named Bernadette Roberts. I devoured it. It stands as one of the most remarkable spiritual autobiographies ever penned. It was an account of her go-to-whoa adventure all the way to experiential union with God and beyond to no-self. I had not seen such a comprehensive and well-written account of the transformative spiritual journey coupled with such an intelligent commentary. Her book *The Path To No Self* was no less impressive. I visited Bernadette in Los Angeles, we had lunch and spent the afternoon together. Again I met her in Australia a few years later. She is currently working on her new book *The Fallacy of Reincarnation*.

By the end of 1996 I had finished dictating the

manuscript for a book called *The Thrill of Mysticism*. A friend, Isabelle Roosenburg had painstakingly typed out thirty hours of tape-recorded monologue. Its progress into print was to be rudely interrupted by some of the startling events that were to follow. The last elements of my self-willed path were beginning to die.

8

BIG SURPRISES

I decided to go into isolation. At the rear of my home was an apartment well suited to this. For thirty years I dreamed of giving myself to a period of exclusive spiritual practice under specific conditions. Perhaps in this way breakthrough was possible. Not having been in isolation before, I wasn't sure how I would respond. To guarantee I wouldn't spit the dummy at the end of day one and leave, I had huge wooden covers crafted to cover the windows and a chute fashioned in one of the doorways through which food could be provided. There was no escape. This was no masochistic venture. The prospect excited me. I was used to marathons of spiritual practice and took delight in it.

I did two ten day stints, one in 1995 and the other in 1996. My day consisted of arising at 4.00 am beginning with ninety minutes of formal meditation, followed by an hour of structured contemplation. Then I would sing the *Guru-Gita*, followed by another chant. That took another ninety minutes. The early morning routine would be finished with forty minutes given over to the spontaneous activities of the awakening. Throughout the day I'd read or rest and do more meditation both formal and spontaneous. My helpful friend Isabelle Roosenburg passed light food through to me twice per day. Never once did I want to leave. All worldly concerns were put behind me. Delighted with the experience I came out after ten days, seeing the world through new eyes. The refreshed perception lasted only for a couple of days.

In early 1996 I repeated the retreat. It was the first day. That afternoon whilst settling myself onto a couch, in a completely plain state of mind, I had a stunning experience. The figure of Jesus Christ formed up within my chest cavity. I was astounded. With the image came the immediate conviction and recognition of who it was. Jesus was standing in a somewhat traditional posture, leaning forward slightly, palms held down and forward. Two seconds following I had a wondrous experience beyond all words can tell. If I were to convey it through the poverty of language: there was an openness to me from Christ of cosmic proportions, and an invitation and a welcome; as if to indicate, 'give me your life and breath and I will take care of you'. I was amazed, delighted, thrilled. The encounter was unmistakable. The message was precise and clear. However, I didn't know what to do with it, since I was rather committed to other spiritual ways. Jesus Christ was worthy of great respect but he was a figure peripheral to my focus.

This experience was equal in marvel to the impersonal penetration of Godhead that I described earlier. Here on the other hand came a wholly personal encounter. It came as a complete surprise. I had in the past identified with and been inspired by the writings and personages of some of the Christian mystic saints, but Jesus had always been a 'flatline'. This had been puzzling. Now he was intimately real.

I carried the memory of this experience around with me for about twelve months. By then I was back in America living in Berkeley, California. Another significant event took place. Over a three-day period, I was overcome by the conviction that my life and spiritual endeavors had added up to a *huge fat zero*. All the years, all the cognitions, realizations and spiritual experiences had been worthless. It was as though I'd been trying to draw water from an empty well. This was no sub-clinical depression; I wasn't having a bad week; I wasn't just thinking things over and coming to this conclusion. This recognition had been pressed into me with great force. It was almost visceral. I was deeply sobered. I'd been reduced to complete zero. All the vibrant charismatic phenomena and thousands of hours of meditation had led nowhere. That was my realization. I thought, 'Oh well, I'll just live out my span and do what I can.' Things began to look simple.

Around this same time, I had been driving from Berkeley to Mill Valley each day. It was a twenty-five minute run and I kept catching evangelical Christian preachers on the radio. Whatever I might have thought of them at first, they were engaging speakers. They had my attention. Listening as the days went by I started to notice connections, at least at this time, between the path of Christianity and the way of the Guru or Siddha Yoga that I'd known so well. I was starting to be educated to the First Principles of Christianity. This was outstanding. I was surprised by some of the insights I was gaining. It was a far deeper look than the 'three bears version' I gleaned from school. At first it was the similarities between Siddha Yoga and Christianity that drew my attention. Then it was the radical differences that became more significant.

So, remembering the vision of Christ and his invitation to me; having been reduced to zero, and therefore having nothing to lose, and now being acquainted with the essentials of the historical Christian faith, I started to get excited about the prospect of accepting Jesus' invitation.

Yes, I was going to do it. But there was to be one intervening event – a last look back of sorts. Three people rang me independently and told me that a young swami was coming to town by the name of Kaleshwar. He was a performer of miracles; the materializations that the guru Sathya Sai Baba is famous for. His charter was to find thirty or forty people who were not wet behind the ears spiritually, who wanted to become teachers and healers in their own right. I wasn't interested. Indian spirituality had

started sounding like a crack in a vinyl record to me.
But three people had invited me. Three. That seemed
a bit beyond coincidence. Perhaps with some remaining belief in synchronicity I thought I should attend –
reluctantly.

Eddy Oliver, a good friend from Siddha Yoga days
was there. He had been a president of the Siddha
Yoga foundation. John Gray of *Men are from Mars
Women are from Venus* fame was there. John and I
had a long chat. He had been the secretary of the
Maharishi Mahesh Yogi of TM fame for years, and
I'd been with Muktananda. Apparently we'd been
next door neighbors, in South Fallsburg where both
gurus had ashrams.

So the swami performed miracles right in my face. I
was sitting next to a man who said, 'I'll believe it
when I see it'. Kaleshwar moved forward and produced *vibhuti*, grey holy ash, from the tips of his
fingers, for him, one foot under my nose. Having
lived in India the land of miracles, for so many years,
this was not so special. I'd seen Sathya Sai Baba do
it, and then I'd scrutinized from the closest range the
woman oozing red *kum-kum* from her fingers at the
rear of the chanting hall in the Ganeshpuri ashram.
Over the course of the days he materialized various
objects. Now this was a bit interesting. These objects
were not actually materialized. They were being
teleported; brought from across any distance in an

177

instant of time. These siddhis or powers were brought about by the power of the word – the use of mantras – as he taught. We were given the elaborate reams of mantras required. It was to take thousands of hours of disciplined practice under particular and demanding conditions for the accomplishment of the skills. It wasn't something for the faint-hearted. Acquiring these abilities didn't interest me. However, the swami did say something that reminded me of something Muktananda had always emphasized in relation to the guru – that is, that faith is essential for spiritual realization. The Swami asked then, 'In whom are you going to have faith?' God was all too general an idea. It had to be a God-man. People made up their mind; the idea was installed in their head, and they went on their way. For me this weekend was a vacuous spiritual event. But the reminding tip on faith had its place.

Now back on track, this resolve to accept Jesus' invitation was going to be the biggest decision of my life. I knew the power, place and importance of decision. I had created a unique training on it. So I wanted to make the decision a memorable event; a marker. I could have made the decision in my sitting room. But that wasn't going to be good enough. It happened that the famous evangelist Billy Graham was coming to town. How surprising. I thought he was dead. What an opportunity to make a decision in the presence of twenty-two thousand witnesses. I went to his grand crusade event *only* for the purpose of making this decision. It was on Sunday, the 28th September, 1997 at approximately 5.35pm that I made that decision. Definitely, cleanly, clearly, - no turning back. It was done.

What followed was extraordinary. From that day to this, I have never been the same. I felt renewed, regenerated. This indeed was a miracle. I would never have credited it. From that day forth all the substantive changes of heart and mind that I had reached-for during a thirty year quest in the Eastern tradition were being given to me by grace as a silent gift of the Holy Spirit.

How did I know? 'By their fruits you shall know them' as the Bible quote goes. I'd been living in a jungle of leafy trees. Now for the first time fruit had appeared. My temperamental disposition and character began to modify. Remarkably I had come to rest. It was not as though I had now found something to believe in, a sort of 'How nice for me'. No. It seemed that for all these years I had been a dead man walking. Now I had come alive. I was not talking out of some honeymoon experience. *The seeker had died.* I'd been swimming about in fine weather and in foul — floating on the surface, treading water, reflecting and philosophizing with friends as we swam, striking out to tranquil inlets, following maps, and hearkening to adventurers' tales — and all of a sudden my feet touched bottom! Wow! — There is a bottom — rest. Now I was established in a peace whose footing lay below experiences and feeling. It was an end, and a new beginning not of my own making.

Looking back I realized that the Berkeley experience of being reduced to zero, was a classic experience of 'repentance from dead works' referred to in the Bible (Hebrews 6:1). This was what it was literally, not just by way of speaking. The word 'repentance' comes from the Greek word *metanoia*. It means a turn or a change, of heart and mind. The about face was not of my doing. And the strong emphasis on repentance was unique to Christianity. It seemed to have been pressed into me. Again it was scripture that pointed to this process. Christ had written on my back. The Holy Spirit had drawn me. As Christ said, 'No one can come to me, unless the Father who sent me draws him' John (6:44). I discovered that this process goes for others, in whatever shape or form, who are in the sights of the Holy Spirit, and that these elements of the process plus others, were specified in scripture.

It was the decision however to *acknowledge* Jesus Christ as Savior and Lord that was the ultimate *turning* point. I had not been evangelized or persuasively converted by Billy Graham on that day, nor had the crusade way of exciting people's interest in the gospel gripped my attention. I had the necessary Biblical understanding on hand before I arrived. It had been the Holy Spirit who had hunted me down and brought me to this point, with pretty much no personal contact with any Christian.

Now I found myself right in the middle of a framework of understanding, that in previous years, I would have considered *ex*oteric churchianity – mere superficial religionism that was nice and helpful for ordinary people, but quite peripheral to serious spirituality.

This renewal was not just an identification with a new set of spiritual concepts. I had not merely taken on a new thought system. I was not an old self made over, repaired or upgraded. There was a sense of being a new creation, for which there was no parallel concept in the Eastern tradition.

The transformation that I experienced, is grounded and explained in the Christian Bible. To date I had thought of the Christian Bible as a book with inspiring parts and wise injunctions but somewhat deficient in spiritual depth. Mind you, I had an opinion about a book I had not properly read!

I tended to be put off by books of faith. I was more interested in works that were thoroughly explained with intellectual clarity and led to *full* understanding leaving little need for faith. Fourth century saint Augustine said (and I noted this long before I became a Christian): 'Seek not to understand that thou mayest believe, but believe that thou mayest understand'. I had definitely preferred it the other way around.

Now this is where the rational bridge was breaking down. Fundamentally, an appreciation for scripture was the product of faith that had now been instilled in me as a gift of grace. But having a grasp of the accurate meaning of its basic terms like law, sin, grace, faith, righteousness, flesh, spirit and others like it, was also important. It was not just a book which contained useful principles found in all religions. It was qualitatively and texturally different, quite distinct from the best works that had held my attention previously.

As the explicit teaching of the Bible became plain, I discerned that the Scripture, the person of Jesus and the Holy Spirit were inextricably linked as the grace evidently working in me. A Holy Spirit. The Holy Spirit? What a gift! What came off the pages was subtly alive to me. It began as a shepherding and cajoling force, spontaneously re-engineering the inclinations which defined my temperament and which had never been amenable to change by any means whatsoever. This hand was new. Quite unfamiliar. I knew what it meant to have intimations for guidance;

intuitions of appropriate action, precognition and the like, but this was quite different. It was a benign, silent shepherd. It was continually inviting me to walk a narrower path, kinder, more real, more moral, less acerbic, and forbearing. And I was starting from *a long* way back. My character was being changed. Self as the center was slowly being dethroned. This was not something occurring under a moral edict, secular or spiritual. It was a force for good that indwelt me at the time of firm decision, which was somehow distinct from the 'gifts' of other paths.

Siddha Yoga and the Eastern tradition were amoral, apart from a casual assent to sensible social mores. The 'do's and don'ts' only existed insofar as they served the self center and its edification. Frankly, I thought Christian mores properly practised were a lovely thing, good for the world, good for society. But I never seriously considered that they were inextricably linked to the transforming core of awareness and truth absolute.

The Eastern texts of substance trivialized the significance of moral decency as *compared* to the ineffable states of being attained by yogis. A new force was at work in me. It seemed to be a comprehensive spiritual force changing my inclinations and constantly inviting behavior to follow. Compared to my old world this was a far cry from self-imposed rectitude which was always impossible to achieve. Utterly impossible.

Now the 'helping hand' was making the impossible possible. I could barely believe it. Progress was slow, but progress was sure. There were on-moments and off-moments, but the drift was always moved by grace towards an exchange from the dissolute and moribund self to the Spirit-controlled life, and consciousness of the new self in relation to Jesus Christ. It was not 'experiential', feeling-based mystical or vibrantly charismatic as had character-ized my journey in the past. It was undramatic, deep and sure. Its promptings were always made known and were gently persuasive. This renewed sense of being benignly cared for, was palpable and encour-aging. Here I speak about a very different order of things than the 'being cared for' in the old paradigm. It was pre-eminent, continuous and overarching and set in a complete and coherent framework of under-standing. And, as it turned out, it was consistent with descriptions in the Bible.

This wasn't merely an extension or a magnification of the old or a fulfillment of something familiar. It was new coin. It wasn't a further development of an already existing evolutionary trajectory. Michael Graham died and a vestigial new being began to arise and take shape.

This all began not after the vision of Christ, or his invitation to me. Nor did it begin after seeing the road I was on had hit a brick wall. It only began at the moment of turning and acknowledging Jesus Christ as Lord and Savior. Those words sound awfully religious, don't they? I'm still not used to talking that way. But that's what happened.

Jesus as Savior added to my life as a lucky charm would have been useless. I needed to add my life to his. Acknowledging him as Lord was the imperative of one half of the equation, acknowledging him as Savior, the other.

The concept of 'Lord', suggested obedience. And this obedience, it seemed to me, would be aligned to the highest good, highest peace, highest truth. It would require heeding what Jesus Christ taught and said by reading the four biographies written about his life by Matthew, Mark, Luke and John.

The word 'obey' means to hear under. That's what a disciple does by definition. I knew that. But now such growing obedience was only possible through the gift of the Holy Spirit, who had come to dwell within me after acknowledging Jesus in the particular way that I did.

I had thought this sort of talk was 'symbolic' in the Bible. Rather, my experience confirmed it as literal.

Again, permanent indwelling only began after the decision, which properly executed, was the most resolute action my consciousness could make. Job done, over, no turning back. I couldn't half-decide. I had either decided or I had not. One couldn't be half pregnant. I had taught this stuff about decision to those who sought to grasp its 'execute–ive' nature.

And what was I deciding about? Obviously I had to be *properly informed* about what I was getting myself into, otherwise there could be a sliding right out of it again. The Bible did that informing along with the aid of *classical* explanatory preaching on its themes.

It was plain that the circumstances that led me to Christ, and indeed the decision itself, occurred under the inspiration and sovereignty of God. The credit goes to Him. My march into Christianity was an unlikely progression from what I had been involved in before.

Even after my long exploration of the world views of the East and 'New Age' movement, in no way was I prepared for the utter newness I was experiencing. Christ was unique it seemed. His concept of person-hood, morality and *reality* were quite different from that of the Eastern tradition. This was not the gnos-tic Christ so sentimentally described by those who had not taken the time to find out what gnosticism was and is, with its life-negative hatred of the flesh and its depreciation of women, as exemplified in the last verse of the 'Gospel of Thomas'. Nor was it the lucky charm wish-fulfilling 'New Age' Christ talked about in the 'New Age' movement, nor the 'Christ Consciousness', but the original, living real Jesus Christ of history, extant right now as the one by whom, through whom and for whom all things were made (Colossians 1:16). To the existence of this one I am able to attest, and to his blessings, having come into full relationship with him.

God and Christ were now at center stage, not as an intellectual idea, but as a sanctifying influence.

This brings me to this born-again phenomenon. I'd met born-again Christians in the past, who had not impressed me. They tended to affirm their reality in my face. Their inability to explain themselves or their terms or at least to point intelligibly in the direction of what they were trying to convey, left me still somewhat curious about the phenomenon of conversion, but not about their particular Christian orientation. Their slipping into religious hyperbole didn't help either.

When in Los Angeles in 1980 I was acquainted in passing with a couple of born-again Christians. I met them on separate occasions. They were bright, articulate and 'normal' in every sense. Our chats would suddenly jump tracks into the born-again Christian thing. It's like they had two brains that were not so well coordinated. My question was, how could someone seem discerning, smart and balanced, yet be talking about this other thing, if there wasn't something in it. I was less dismissive at this point. They were neither clinically insane nor liars. And they both appeared as buoyant and happy people. It intrigued me since I was curious about all spiritual matters. It remained in the back of my mind as one of those unanswered questions – very far back, but in no way would I have considered following up.

Years later when the re-birth took place in me I knew exactly what they were talking about! I was born-again. Yikes, I am embarrassed to say it, simply because it's not generally understood. It's unfathomable, even nonsense to one who does not have the eyes to see. I mean this respectfully, not in a derisive or superior way. But what I hadn't tasted I couldn't know.

In John chapter three, Nicodemus a Jewish religious leader inquired of Jesus 'What must I do to enter the kingdom?' Jesus replied, 'You must be born-again'. This puzzled Nicodemus who thought he was referring to re-entering his mother's womb which he knew was impossible. Jesus reassured him that he meant born-again of the Spirit, or born from above.

Interesting! There could have been no better description of what happened to me, and what I can still attest to years down the track. This wasn't Biblical mystery talk; it was an actual thing.

Some people would have one believe that the Bible is principally allegorical or symbolic. As I read, it became not so to me. I found it comprehensive and revelatory, with a living quality, quite unlike even the most sophisticated spiritual tomes contrived by human minds. It states that Jesus asserted to his immediate disciples that the Holy Spirit would teach them all things and bring to their remembrance all that he taught (John 14:26). And it was written, inspired by the Holy Spirit and declares that 'All scripture is God-breathed and profitable for teaching, for reproof, for correction, for instruction in true goodness, that the man of God may be complete, thoroughly equipped for every good work.' (2 Timothy 3:16). The Bible was all-confirming itself to me in experience. It was not a book of dead but interesting informative data, but became the way through which the Holy Spirit communicated with me.

An appreciation of the Holy Spirit-driven-Biblical Christian way, and the fruit of spiritual regeneration came as a homogeneous amalgam. It wasn't as though I took a bit here and left a bit there. It was a pleasure to embrace. It was a new life, with a new purpose, and new meaning, not merely imbibed through a series of intellectual conclusions. But its

189

significance was pressed upon me from a now new indwelling Spirit. It was not mental assent but a form of the fruit of faith – a faith of which I was not the author and I'm jolly sure, not the finisher. Thank goodness. All was being accomplished through grace, compliance being elegantly prompted and supported by the Holy Spirit in all that God requires of me in coming to his likeness from *however far back*.

I appreciated that the salvation that the Bible promises means to be salvaged, a bit like salvaging or rescuing a sunken boat from the depths of the sea. Jesus Christ was disclosed as Savior and divinely acts to salvage us. From what? From the inexorable consequences of our decision to separate from God. That's called 'sin'. We live under the inherited primordial momentum of this decision for separation from which we are unable to be freed save by grace alone, by faith alone, in Jesus Christ.

Amidst all this, it's tricky to explain the qualitative and textual distinction of the 'rest' and peace I now experience. It contrasts with the spiritual experiences of the past, that may have been described in similar terms, though the word 'rest' would never have been one among them.

I captured the difference while talking to someone on the phone the other day. Have you ever lost your

car keys or eye glasses? You have an appointment at
4.00 pm. Its 3.30 pm and you're heading for the
door of your home. Suddenly you realize you don't
have your glasses and you have an important document to read at the meeting. So you start looking for
them. They are not in any of the usual places.
Standing in the hallway you take pause. Now let me
think. Think. Where could I have left them? You
check a couple more spots. Darn. Where are they?
Time is running out. I hate to be late. Then you start
thinking; worse, those glasses will cost two hundred
dollars to replace. Once more you rack your brains
and take possession of your wits. Deliberately again,
you look in two places very carefully. And then,
voila! – almost by chance you spot them. Phew! The
relief is palpable. Really palpable. You let out a sigh.
Done. Then you go on your way. Anyone can relate
to that with glasses or keys. Most people *live in*
'Where are my keys?' or 'Where are my glasses?'
but they barely realize it. The dilemmas of life are
rationalized. Coming to rest in Christ was *living in*
PHEW. No, it wasn't just a lovely little belief system. It was a coming to REST in the way, the truth
and the life. I'd known ineffable states and an impersonal abiding. But this was different. It remained
beyond words, but not those ones. Those experiences were subtle jazz.

I no longer looked to marvelous spiritual experiences as being so significant. It was all over in

Christ. My life was added to his. Not his to mine. All that was left to do was to enjoy the done work of Christ. The end was known from the beginning, but the beginning had to catch up. Called at eleven, touched at fifteen, moved at twenty-two, envisioned at forty-eight, salvaged at fifty. It was after salvation that sanctification began.

I learned that sanctification is the *process* of renewal that takes place through the influence of the Holy Spirit. It's characterized by a change of heart, mind and inclinations, unachievable through strategic means. The Holy Spirit 'leads us into all truth' (John 16:13). It was not a 'Wow, I'm now tumbling through the universe backwards' type of thing that was the yield of mysticism. It was the beginning of a renewal with implications through the full spectrum of life on both sides of the mystery. It was planted in the bedrock of ultimate truth, not in the ephemeral and revolving phantasmagoria of experiences.

Where does it end? In glorification, it is said. That's the Biblical term. It's sometimes difficult to elicit sparks of recognition from this terminology because notions like salvation, sanctification and glorification among many others which have disappeared right out of common usage, were identified by me with quaint notions from antiquity. And they don't have exact equivalents in the Eastern tradition or the 'New Age' movement. I've had to make the adjustment. But now the terms remain pregnant with meaning.

Biblically, 'glorification' means we become partakers in the divine nature absolutely. We become as Christ and apperceive him as he is. And we can take all this out way beyond word definition.

I learned that salvation, sanctification and glorification take place by grace through faith alone in Jesus Christ, and not by works (Ephesians 2:8-9). That is, not by any inventive means no matter how clever; not by self-effort, not by massive discipline, not by meritorious acts or by charitable works. These features however may become the fruit of our 'faith of which Jesus Christ is the author and finisher' (Hebrews 12:2) – the external evidence of the fruit of the Spirit.

The cross of Jesus Christ was a monumental puzzle to me too. After all some of the best minds of history believed in it. I must have been missing something. And this puzzlement existed even after I became a Christian. Its meaning and significance were elusive, but enlightening as understanding and appreciation dawned.

Surprisingly the general concept was not completely new. The way of the Siddha Guru has a *similar* but not *identical* notion. The guru takes on a person's

193

karma, being the consequences of their actions. The guru sometimes takes upon his body some of the person's *karma*, thus freeing them from some of the consequences of actions. It's a small-scale thing. If Baba Muktananda had a stomach ache, people might be overheard saying, 'Oh Baba's taking on such-and-such *karma*'. I was always skeptical of this sort of thing. But here we had Jesus Christ on the cross, who in one cosmic gesture, took on within his body the entire *'karma'* of the world, the gift of which is appropriated by those who turn to Him in acknowledgement. This *'karma'* is the inescapable collective momentum of the decision to turn from God, leaving us eternally trapped and separated from Him. However, using Eastern concepts to interpret the cross of Christ falls short, since the Christian understanding enjoins some distinct differences.

The turning away from God partly consists of doing what's right in our *own* eyes, spiritually or otherwise. As the Bible goes, 'There is a way that seems *right* to a man, but in the end leads to death' (Proverbs 14:12). That I learned was the anatomy of sin – doing our *own* thing regardless.

By flying in the face of the way things were *designed* to be, serious consequences follow, to which everyone stuck in the human condition can partly attest — yet without cognition of the eternal consequences.

And so we hear that it was the God-ordained-sacrificial-act-of-Christ Himself that plucks us out of the jaws of this kind of death. It was accomplished by Jesus' complete identification with sin. As the text goes, 'He became sin', though not a sinner, and by so doing fully consumed sin for our release. Jesus' puzzling statement on the cross: 'My God, My God, why have you forsaken me?' now became clear; an eternal bond of love that had existed before time's beginning became momentarily broken — broken between two persons of the one God, Father and Son. It's understood that sin with all its self-justifying forms cannot admix with the impeccability of Godhead.

We can learn that in this act of sacrifice for the love of lost mankind, the assurance of salvation (salvage) was struck, along with the means for transformation for those who are non-dismissive and who recognize and *hold* to Christ's redemptive work.

In the context of the entire Biblical account from the book of Genesis to the book of Revelation, it is apparent that at the point of Jesus' atoning death, a new once-and-for-all principle of release broke into creation. Again it was added for those who bowed their knee in acknowledgement of and belief in 'the one whom God had sent' (John 6:29). It was added and functioned at the same level through which the entire creation was declared, or decided into existence. It was the principle of salvation/liberation through faith by means of Jesus Christ through grace alone. No less than the creator Himself, stepped down into human flesh as Jesus Christ, could consume in one gesture of sacrifice, the whole groaning momentum of everlasting entrapment caused by our decision to turn from God and from His ways.

In sharing my conversion to Christianity I have taken a few logical leaps for which no gradient arguments have been presented. Alas those steps are beyond the scope of this book. I may now be starting to sound like those Christians who had so *un*impressed me before. What to do? Remember that Saint Paul said that all this stuff sounded like 'foolishness to the Greeks' – the clever ones. Here I have lighted on a few of the First Principles of the Christian Way as I have understood them from scripture without going into long chains of convincing argument.

I had not gone mad or entered a pollyanna world. Life went on and good days and bad days remained. However as a Christian, my worst day contained an intangible quality that was absent completely from best day pre-Christ. This added value was not merely an interpretative overlay that provided solace in difficult situations. I was now deeply anchored in something beneath thinking, feeling or experience. Indeed this was a new life. I was led to an unexpected conclusion and a radical reversal. The form of this enlightenment was surprising. Tantalized by the sophistry of Eastern metaphysical thought systems and experiences, I would never have guessed that coming to rest in the simplicity that is Christ would yield a substance and calm beneath appearances superior to the most exalted mystic revelations. This was a knowingness beyond intellect and wordiness. It cannot be argued for. It's known by grace alone. Indeed, this became so to me. 'For it is by grace you have been saved, through faith – and this not from yourselves, it is the gift of God' (Ephesians 2:8).

I walk in gratitude. As time takes me further from the point of renewal, that which was so surprising is becoming instead familiar. The immediate appreciation of comparative value is waning. My memories as regards the old life are thinning.

The path grows narrower as I walk. The relinquishments that are asked of me require no sacrifice, just a tension at the point of relinquishment, since what replaces the leavings-off, is a deeper and more fruitful walk with God.

9
A NEW BEGINNING

I ask myself what the new life is like, and how its nuances might be communicated to make sense. There are so many elements to it which are indeed new. Chief among them is the cajoling, the shepherding, the leading of the Holy Spirit.

Once I might have thought of the Holy Spirit as an exclusively charismatic feature – a visitation, an energy, a voice, a discernible tugging. But this Holy Spirit, the third person of the Trinity, consisting of the Father, the Son and the Spirit, operated quietly for me with only unusual promptings showing up through spiritual experiences. This new indwelling guide could renew one's life without experiences or peculiar feelings being involved. His work was recognized in retrospect.

I believe spiritual experiences remain legitimate and could be thought of as icing on a cake, but not the cake itself. But it was refreshing to know that substantive spiritual progress was not predicated on feelings or spiritual experiences at all, but wrought undramatically.

Fruit there had to be. Some evidence of change needs to be discerned. What, otherwise, would be the point of spiritual life if nothing shifted. The fruit showed up as a gradual softening of my disposition, a changing of inclinations, and a changing of my temperament and character. It was noticeable to me. It may or may not have been noticeable to others, but some recognized it. My son noticed it. That was good enough for me. And yes, there was a bit of backsliding.

It had always been my own vices and shortcomings that aggrieved me most. So often, I willed the right and did the wrong. My best intentions were spoiled in this way, and were overshadowed by an inclination to run counter to them.

I had been attracted to the whole Eastern Quest by the promise of a life free of suffering and an experiential union with the Highest Reality. But equally I had been unsatisfied with the way I was. I had sought change for the better. I discovered that some of my compatriots from the old world had never undertaken spiritual activity with a view to changing. They had other motives. Perhaps some were self-satisfied? For some, no internal monitor was apparent that assessed their character or conduct as they moved. Was conscience moribund? Certainly for me conscience became more alive in Christ. For some, lifestyle was a motive, for others, community, yet for others, ambition. The need to feel loved by a Guru figure was an imperative for many and for others it was enough to be rapt in solipsistic experiences. Some were contented with superstition or a belief that kept them satisfied. Few probably were driven by a quest for Truth.

Recently I read that Francis Shaeffer, one of the better thinkers of the last fifty years, stated, 'There are only two types of people; those who seek for truth and those who seek for self-justification'. That I thought was a mighty distinction. Thinking into it, I found that the forms and implications of self-justification were enormous. Some systems even institutionalize and deify it. Anyway, I took self-*dis*satisfaction as an attribute, unlike the pundits of psychologism who exhort one to high self-regard, merited or not.

And I considered that the entire creation must turn on one Absolute Truth. After all, if gravity had bricks falling at a terminal velocity of one-hundred-and-eighty feet per second and that was a fact, why couldn't the most fundamental fact of all be discovered and appreciated.

The quest for this Absolute was *impersonally* fulfilled as a young man, when I was annihilated in the unnamable 'Godhead'. And this Absolute Truth was *personally* fulfilled in my encounter with Jesus Christ. And it was most significantly fulfilled, in his Spirit entering me later, along with the reading of his Biblical word.

So the Holy Spirit was doing a measurable work. I was pleased with such a correction of the wayward me. It seemed more of a miracle than the highest experience of cosmic consciousness. How grateful I was. The Bible declares that the Holy Spirit leads us into all truth (John 16:13) and convicts us of sin (John 16:8). This means that it convinces us of our missing the mark and our reprobation and complete need of the saving hand of Christ's grace.

I like Tal Brook's comment from his book *The other side of Death*. 'The Hebrew word for 'sin', *Chartha* means 'go wide of the mark', which can mean to miss it by only a hair. But in essence, sin is a constant preference for the assertions or intuitions of self, over the proclamations of God.'

Importantly, sin's omissions and commissions are significant because they stifle and distort our consciousness of God and His will.

The concept of sin is subsidiary in the religious systems that declare 'I am Brahman', ('Ahambrahmasmi') or 'He I am' which refers to the 'divine' inner Self as the impeccable Holy Absolute.

Part of the turning from ignorance has to do with embracing the very opposite of what these Eastern systems propound. For example, I found that it was most liberating to recognize my own hopelessness, rather than ratcheting up my self-regard to narcissistic proportions in order to accommodate the pundits of psychologism, or even dovetail myself into the munificent status of 'I am God' according to the Hindu Vedantins and Kashmir Shaivites.

By reputation and in view of the fundamentals of Hindu and Buddhist thought, (the yogas), it is not surprising to me that senior luminaries in the Eastern tradition manifest exceedingly elastic ethics across the full range of human activity. It's a fact. These luminaries are not mere pastors, priests or clergymen, bishops or cardinals. They declare their own enlightenment and act as Saviors and grand preceptors in their own right. They can declare one thing and do another. They are the ones into whose hands many place their faith and hope, and the fate of the world. How wise is this? Yet, in other ways, these characters often appear to be extraordinary people with a salutary side.

In the more mature Christians I'd met, I saw a level of loving-kindness, giving and decency that was exemplary. They had embraced Jesus' ethics as the God-given values we need to imbibe and enact every day (e.g. Sermon on the Mount, Matthew 5-7). It was clear that this couldn't be done without the empowering Spirit of Christ himself, dwelling in and with us through and in the person of the Holy Spirit. It was an implacable direction that I didn't see manifest in the other paths I'd known. This was noteworthy and distinctive.

After one year into my Christian walk, I was still teaching meditation. I was an accomplished meditator. I had been enjoying an increasing clientele, and I liked the work of teaching meditation. It gave me some sort of a living too. A doctor friend of mine, Danny Lewis, had been referring patients and colleagues to me for tuition. As the numbers increased, and as I became more gratified by the expansion of this clientele, so did I become more uneasy – but for a strange reason. I was being moved to drop all this work. I was stuck in a dilemma, but a pleasantly significant spiritual one. Early I recognized that I was being invited by the Holy Spirit to relinquish this technique or 'works-based' Eastern *mantra*-style of meditation, and by so doing, demonstrate that I truly believed in the *sufficiency* of Christ 'in whom are hid *all* the treasures of wisdom and knowledge' (Colossians 2:3). It was to be Christ plus nothing. Not Christ plus meditation, not Christ plus personal development; not Christ plus techniques. This was difficult but exciting. I finally made the declaration, 'That's it!' and dumped the lot.

In the process of getting to that point, I had twisted and turned my understanding in every way to justify this meditation work. It didn't work. The Spirit was relentless. Much to the surprise of many, I quit. The demonstration had been made. All was well. It's another quiet and persistent way the Holy Spirit worked on me.

Still being a bit resistant to the decision I had made under the prompting of the Holy Spirit, I put my toe back into the personal meditation water as an experiment. Each time, for the three or four days that followed, my walk became discombobulated – ruffled. The spirit was relentless.

My old spiritual practices were replaced by prayer; but not with the same motive. This was communication, not technique centered on self. Though salvation takes place by grace alone, everything doesn't stop there. We are exhorted by Christ in scripture to acknowledge God, appreciate God, to acknowledge His divine truth and make our requests known to Him. Prayer seems to be a God-ordained manner in which providence works towards the good and is causally connected to outcomes desired by God, his devotee, and those of his people.

In Luke 11:1-4 Jesus' disciples ask Jesus 'Teach us to pray'. The theme recurs incessantly in scripture; I'm sure for good reason.

After giving up the teaching of meditation, I was left with nothing to do – seriously on the couch, so to speak. I had been a technique plus 'grace'-

dispensing monger. Now there were no supplements to add to the sufficiency I had found in Christ. After months of dead stop nothing regards professional activity, Sydney theologian, Philip Johnson heard of my story. He was in Melbourne and we spent several hours in conversation. Philip had made it a theological specialty to talk into the world views of alternate spiritualities, looking to create, for those seekers, a bridge back to the Gospel. He thought my story uncommon and engaging, and one that needed to be told. Philip is gratefully acknowledged at the front of this book and he has written the forward to it.

Following our conversation, Philip arranged for me to be interviewed by Gordon Moyes out of the Sydney Opera House on Easter Sunday morning at a service televised on national station Seven. What followed were several engagements including interviews on two Sydney-based secular radio stations, and two talks including question and answers with the students at the Baptist and Presbyterian theological colleges in Sydney. Following this, I was interviewed by the Christian SCP journal in the United States and had several write-ups in Christian periodicals. It was also a great privilege to be invited by Pastor Jossy Chacko to India to speak before twenty-five thousand Christians in Navapur, and by Pastor Chris Williams to address students at the Union Biblical Seminary and other groups, in Pune. All this came as a surprise to me, as my personal will seemed not to be involved. These appointments were a gift of grace, and a delight to offer as I was able to testify to the saving grace of Jesus Christ that I had by then known.

A further joy to me was my son's conversion to Christianity. He was born into Siddha Yoga, and was given special attention by Muktananda. He spent years in India. At the age of twenty he acknowledged Jesus Christ as Lord and Savior. His approach to Jesus Christ had begun four years earlier, independent of my own. Since my conversion two years earlier, I had shared with him on many hours of taped letters all the details and nuances of my Christian walk – teachings, thoughts, considerations and comparisons. We had shared in our approaches the schooling of top expository preaching of the classical variety – no water added. To these men we are grateful.

It was at the end of a one hour international telephone call that Yogiraj announced to me, 'I've given my life to Christ!' I was intrigued, on three occasions before, knowing that he was schooling himself on the first principles of the faith, I'd asked him, 'Are you ready to decide and turn?' Each time he had confessed, 'I can't put Christ at the center of my life – yet.' Apparently, the pressing of the Holy Spirit changed that.

One day, at the end of two months of life-unraveling experiences, he drove away from home reflective. He knew 'Yogiraj has to be buried.' He stopped, walked through a graveyard into the forest, where he prayed for clarity and conviction. Passing through the tombstones again, he continued on his drive. The clarity and conviction prayed for dawned upon him. He pulled over his car, and as he put it to me 'at 7:47 pm on the first of July, I turned. I made the decision to acknowledge Jesus Christ as Lord and Savior. His own story unfolds. He reflects now that he had actually 'crossed the line' before making that formal decision. When, he wasn't sure. Nor did it matter. A new life was his.

The Bible indicates that the Christian way is life affirmative. Life is not suffering to be transcended, or an illusion to be seen through, not even a play of consciousness to be enjoyed, or an evolutionary trajectory, but a brilliant design whose form and content is in the process of being undistorted and brought to perfection along with us under grace. The design covers the entire panoply of the created order both seen and unseen. It is of our Infinite Source and it enjoys its beginning, middle and end in Christ. It is a huge gestalt existing under the sovereignty of God. Properly positioned and in right relationship to God through Christ, the personal quest ends. All motivations are dried up. The nagging that propels the search is gone.

As Saint Augustine said, 'Thou hast made us for Thyself, O Lord, and our hearts are restless until they rest in Thee.' That rest is found in Christ.

10
REFLECTIONS

Reflections have inevitably followed this spiritual odyssey. It seems that I had not really come out of the 'New Age' movement mainly. It was more of an alternative Old Age movement from which I came – 'Hinduism', Vedantic and yogic ways and philosophies – the sort of thing the traditional gurus taught. I did however, seek to supplement my core endeavors with explorations into the human potential branch of the 'New Age' style spirituality to see if there was anything there that worked.

It is probably not inaccurate to state that today's popular broad spectrum spirituality and its presuppositions *mainly* stem from convenient selections from parts of the Hindu thought system presented under different labels. This world view was given legs to the West by theosophists in the mid-1800s and was capped off by the Indian Swami invasions of the 1970s and 1980s. There are some exceptions of course, like 'native earth' religions which are becoming increasingly popular. The 'New Age' movement is actually so diverse that one person described the difficulty of defining it as trying to nail jelly to a wall.

With there being over two-hundred-and-thirty-one ways to grow, each ascribing a different cause for your 'problem', and each prescribing a different 'solution', it often seemed to me more of a mess than something useful. Each person was invited to believe what he or she liked. Two plus two equals four. 'How do you *feel* about that?' – is the way the thinking went. 'Well, does it really matter how you feel about it?' Hmmm. I really couldn't see how people could get excited about so many seeming contradictions. However within that pile of possibilities there were some observations of interest.

Reflections arising from this seeming world of confusion led to my developing a presentation called 'The Anatomy of Believing'. I thoroughly enjoyed giving this talk. It set out to expose and deconstruct the kind of thinking described above. I was disseminating this information ten years before I became a Christian.

The contemporary popular end of the 'New Age' movement with its *focus* on divination, astrology, channeling, organic brown rice, magic, visualizations, lovely meditations and so many other things, held little of my attention. Those five Great Spiritual Traditions that had stood the test of time each had their 'New Age' movements on their periphery. These interests were thought to be ancillary and distracting to the fundamental quest. 'New Agers' were worshipping the rocks, rather than that or whom from which the rocks came into existence.

So, by the middle of my search the distinction

between phenomena and the ground from which it arose became important to me.

In bringing me to Christ, the Holy Spirit, working in my intuition, interested me in seeking an accurate and simple crucible of understanding into which to place my faith – a truth independent of what my 'itching ears may have wanted to hear' (2Timothy 4:3).

It made sense to be properly informed. A lot was at stake. And mind you, I was not to be disappointed. Christ had written on my back. The Spirit has hunted me down. It was after I became a Christian that I went yet deeper into the arguments which I found intellectually satisfying, pried through sophisticated reasonings and scrutinized evidence. It seemed that in the Christian Biblical overview I had found the most plausible big and small picture rationale or explanation for the history, purpose and conditions of humankind – who, what and why we are, from whence we'd come, where we are now and where we are going.

By contrast the Eastern explanations, thought into and thought through, seemed wanting. A light look would not have yielded this appreciation of the contrast.

And what I learned about the Christian way was a far

cry from the superficial and ill-educated comments one sometimes hears about Christianity out there in the press or in the 'spiritual market place'.

At this point it's beyond the scope of this story to do any more than offer some simple reflections, and affirm some further truths, rather than fully explain them.

After my encounter with Christ, and during my education to the first principles of biblical Christianity, I was drawn by the similarities between elements of the Eastern spiritual tradition, particularly Siddha Yoga and Christianity. I soon thereafter realized that it was *not* the similarities that were significant, but the differences.

In certain forms of Yogic Hindu Philosophy, the pinnacle of enlightenment is the experiential recognition of the divine inner self as identical with God. This is summarized by the great statement 'I am God'. In Christianity God's splendor will be revealed *in* us (as indicated in Romans 8:18), but God and man remain ultimately different levels of being. Yet indeed, all people are made in the image and likeness of God and are *through Christ,* brought into personal relationship with him, saved and transformed to be partakers of the divine nature.

Almost fully so in Buddhism and half so in Hindu

Yogic philosophy, self-effort is the pure means of salvation/liberation. But according to classical biblical Christianity taken as the inspired word of God, salvation/liberation is accomplished as a gift of grace alone, appropriated through faith alone, because of Jesus Christ, alone. Salvation is all of God and *none* of self. Any self, no matter how exalted, is impotent to achieve salvation. Even the *necessary* motivation to self-effort is of grace. This is unique, and it is the good news (which means Gospel) in its shortest form.

It is understood in biblical Christianity that a deep flaw has so tarnished all parts of our self (not merely ego) that there is nothing of this fallen creation that we are, that can aid and abet salvation. All apparent personal volition and effort in this direction is a gift from God, though it may *seem* to arise from ourselves.

Again we are literally *declared* saved by God through faith in Jesus Christ from the same level of omnipotence from which the creation of the universe was postulated. This is a once and for all salvation through a *declaration* of God. Christianity starts with salvation. Other classical systems *seek* to end with it. By their own admission it is rarely obtained.

This eternal status of salvation is accredited to us by our acknowledging Jesus Christ as Lord and Savior.

Through this acknowledgement and by *turning* (repentance) Christ's impeccable standing before God then becomes ours and grants open-eyed access to the work of His Spirit.

As the U-turn took place, there was a move from finding sufficiency in self, to finding sufficiency in Him, gradually through the turn of the U. It is as though weaknesses and limitations were given so that self-sufficiency would fail and the recognition of Him as being the source of our supply would dawn.

Believing that in Him are contained *all* the treasures of wisdom and knowledge (Colossians 2:3) and being willing to demonstrate reliance on that sufficiency required a relinquishment of all other spiritual investments.

Some fundamental differences between Eastern Mysticism and Christianity were significant to me. The Eastern Godman seeks to ascend to God leaving behind his carnal self and disappearing into the raptures of unearthly states of being or to enjoy radically altered states of wakeful awareness. Even the Hindu *avatar* comes to earth and returns home again without mixing it in the difficult grist of earthliness. On the other hand, according to *Biblical* revelation, Christ, as God impeccable, stepped down into human flesh to share the nature of both man and God simultaneously and took on the nature of a servant.

He was also exposed to all temptations. He succumbed to none. He further descended at the point of His atoning death into total identification with sin absolute (not His but ours) to the point of momentary loss of connection with the Father as He cried 'My God, My God, why have you forsaken me?' (Matthew 27:46). So while the Easterner reaches up to find God, Christ stoops down to find and salvage us from the mire. This was how God expressed His love for us through the person of Jesus, in His death and in His physical resurrection. It alone was a gesture of love for the purpose of reconciliation of man with his creator. There was a principle involved. It could be done no other way. Behind it was love.

Central to the Christian revelation, is the understanding that it was through the atoning death of Jesus Christ on the Cross that the entire momentum of world sin was consumed or broken for those alone who acknowledge Jesus Christ as Lord and Savior – who believe in Him. Again salvation all happens at the level of declaration, fundamentally from God's side not ours. It does not take place from the level of our own efforts or techniques which so characterize some forms of mysticism under various labels.

Such a means of salvation can barely be believed by the smart, the clever and the worldly-wise. The scales of recognition only fall from our eyes if the Holy Spirit, even prior to our conversion, has us in

215

his sights. That's why Saint Paul, the ex-elite crack troop Pharisee Patrician Religionist Kabalist and Scholar, counted all his great spiritual practices and discernments as dung, (literally), after discovering the simplicity in Christ and Him crucified (Philippians 3:8).

Well before this point, most of my old fellow-travelers on the Eastern path may well be yawning. What can I say? Being in Christ leaves me amazed, grateful and most surprised all at once. I'd swap it for nothing. As it says in Paul's letter to the Corinthians, the Christian way is a stumbling block to the Jews and foolishness to the Greeks (1Corinthians 1:23). In other words, a stumbling block to works and ritual-based religionists and sheer simplistic idiocy to the *world's* clever and wise. Christianity is not the product of wise men using their limited minds and limited senses to make limited observations and draw limited conclusions within a limited reality to come up with insights about how life works and what it is all about. Christianity is a supernaturally-revealed religion. Again, what I now see as so valuable, I would have once branded mere 'Churchianity', as compared to the sophistry of other metaphysical systems.

My old way could fairly be described as a form of 'gnosticism': being the 'secret' and 'superior' way. Saint Paul and Christ's disciple Peter bent over backwards to keep the pure teaching of Jesus Christ from being polluted by the adjunct of gnostic mysticism as a means separate from the pure grace of God through Jesus Christ.

With the advent of Christ, God's truth and His way of doing things broke into our world in a new way. Jesus said, 'You will know the (this) truth and the truth will set you free' (John 8:32). And so now, the person of Jesus Christ and scripture are inextricably linked as the special reveal-ation of the Spirit of God.

With twenty-eight years of vibrant charismatic spiritual phenomena behind me as a measure of comparison, I know the great distinctive found in Christ – the rest and sufficiency we find in him, through simple faith by grace and the revelation of the Bible. Never would I limit the grace of the Holy Spirit by affirming that mystical revelation or experiences were not given as grace to some. However to volitionally seek salvation through the *primary* means of charismatic phenomena or mystical revelation or the cultivation of religious ecstasy is, I believe, a form of spiritual materialism that endlessly misleads. Pure phenomena. The numinous is not found in this. Mysticism can so easily become a false measure of spirituality.

Again, I found that those who predicated their spiritual lives and progress on spiritual experiences or feelings (and I included myself in this) and pursue curiosities that endlessly emerge from varieties of spiritual alternatives, build their lives on an unstable or shaky foundation – sand. Peace and stability rest in acknowledging, meditating upon and heeding the teachings and precepts of Jesus Christ and his apostles as found in the New Testament. Cleaving to these abiding truths in faith and seeking to obey, gives us the foundations of truth – rock – which under grace, grounds us beyond mere assent to a new set of beliefs.

This is the New Millenium. Such stories never go out of date. What is next in the unfolding life of one Christian man? I am not sure. There will be more surprises no doubt. Gratitude and expectancy walk me on.

Decades of experiential participation in Eastern mysticism, the world of personal development and the 'New Age' movement, have led me to believe that there is nothing to compare in value with classical Biblical Christianity. Every truth finally leads to Christ. In him the crown is found, the picture complete, and the *full* means of salvation given. As told in the Bible, love is behind the whole redemptive history of the relationship between the creator (God) and the created (humankind), all fulfilled in Christ. Christ's absolute openness to and acceptance of me was made clear in a personal encounter, just as his acceptance and promise can be made plain to anyone, through proper examination of promises in the New Testament. Christ gave more credit to someone who believes without having 'seen' when he said, 'Blessed are those who have not seen and yet have believed' (John 20:29).

The free love of God in Christ is the jumping-off point. Faith follows as does repentance. Repentance is turning from a previous way; an 'about face'.

This whole-hearted decision to repent of old investments is not merely mental assent to a new set of religious propositions, but involves a mystery, a rebirth into a new life, God-given and of grace alone. This is all silliness to natural wisdom – all too simplistic. Yet it is what is asked of us. Jesus Christ asked it of us – the miracle follows.

Michael Graham

U-turn, further turn

NOTES ABOUT WRITTEN SOURCES:

Some references to Michael Graham can be found in various publications, particularly in the publicly available literature of Siddha Yoga. During Muktananda's lifetime the Ganeshpuri ashram published an annual periodical called *Shree Gurudev Vani*. Michael is referred to, or contributions by him, may be seen in the following:

* A letter by Michael appeared in Volume 7 July 1970, p 74. He is also listed as a visitor to the Ganeshpuri ashram on p 82 of the same issue.

* A report on Muktananda's first Australian tour records that Michael met him at Sydney airport in Volume 8 July 1971, p 99.

* An article by Michael, 'The Two Wings' was published in Volume 16 July 1979, pp 99-104.

* After Muktananda 's first Australian tour, a book was published to commemorate it. Michael is mentioned on p 17, and a photograph of Michael with Swami Muktananda appears on p 54. See, *Swami Muktananda Paramahansa in Australia*, published; Shree Gurudev Meditation Center, Melbourne, 1971.

* Muktananda's second tour of Australia, 1975, was commemorated by the publication of the book Sadgurunath Maharaj Ki Jay. A picture of Michael appears on page 74

* Muktananda recounts the awakening experienced by an unnamed Australian businessman in *Where Are You Going?* published by SYDA Foundation, New York, 1981, p 68. It is a thumbnail sketch of Michael's experience.

* Michael was interviewed as a teacher of the *Avatar®* program for an article by Diana Bagnall, 'Soul Food City of the South', *The Bulletin*, July 14, 1992, pp 46-48.

* Michael appears in the documentary film *The Die Hard: The Legend of Lasseter* Narrated by James Mason

GLOSSARY

* *Ashram*: Sanskrit. A center for meditation or religious study. A monastery, hermitage. A place for spiritual practice.

* *Ashtavakra*: Sanskrit, lit. 'deformed in eight places'. The sage who defined some of the teachings and insights of *Vedanta* in his song/poem the Ashtavakra Gita.

* *Avadhut*: Sanskrit. An enlightened one who lives beyond all conventions and ties to the world.

* *Avatar:* Sanskrit, lit. 'descent' - a divine incarnation sent to lay a spiritual pathway fitting for the age in which he comes.

* *Bhagavad Gita*: Sanskrit lit. song of the holy one. It is considered to be the Hindu 'Bible'. A teaching poem.

* *Bhajan*: Sanskrit, worship of God with singing or music.

* *Bhakti*: Sanskrit, a yogic path of ardent devotion to God through love and surrender to God or guru, often leading to states of ecstatic adoration.

* *Chakra*: Sanskrit, lit. 'circle or wheel'. Refers to subtle energy centers through which body and soul intersect and which are purified through the activity of the Kundalini. Seven *chakras* are located along the axis of the spine from its tip to the crown of the head.

* *Fana*: Islamic *Sufi* term meaning 'annihilation in God'.

* *Gita*: Sanskrit, lit. 'song'. The word commonly refers to *Bhagavad Gita*. There are other religious songs such as *Ashtavakra Gita, Avadhuta Gita, Guru Gita* etc.

* *Guru*: spiritual master or guide. Anyone from parents, to worldly teacher, to a spiritual preceptor, to a god-man or avatar.

* *Hatha Yoga*: the means to God through body life-breath. See Yoga.

* *Japa:* Sanskrit, repetition of sacred word, formula or mantra

* *Jnana*: Sanskrit, knowledge of ultimate truth. The path of intellectual discrimination that leads to illumination and release from the spell of *Maya*.

* *Karma*: Sanskrit, lit. 'deed, action'. The principle of reaping what you sow in terms of happy or sorrowful consequences. Implications also extend from past, present, future lives.

* *Kashmir Shaivism:* An important but lesser known Indian

philosophy. It postulates the idea that the world is a projection of supreme consciousness and unlike *vedanta*, real as it appears. A non-renunciation philosophy.

* *Kriya*: Sanskrit, lit. 'operation or deed'. Used in Siddha Yoga to denote the spontaneous operation of shakti or *Kundalini* most often referring to physical manifestations.

* *Kum Kum:* Red dry powder often mixed into a paste to apply to Hindu women's forehead as a religious symbol.

* *Kundalini*: Sanskrit, lit. 'serpent power'; coiled divine energy dormant at the bottom of the spine. It awakens and arises through the Chakra system to the crown of the head bringing illumination or god-union. It is also termed, Kundalini-Shakti.

* *Mala:* Sanskrit, lit. 'garland'. String of prayer beads used for *mantra* repetition and sometimes worn around the neck.

* *Mantra*: Sanskrit, lit. a name for God and the word embodiment of the guru's teaching. It is a power word repeated for purification or spiritual progress.

* *Maya*: Sanskrit, lit. appearance, illusion, deception. The veiling force that makes us perceive the world as real. *Maya* is the force that obscures our perception of the One Reality and leads us to erroneously view the world of mind and matter as real. It is projected from the Absolute (Brahman). It is a key concept of Vedanta by which Maya's deceptive influence on awareness is dispelled.

* *Muktananda*: Sanskrit, lit. 'the bliss of freedom'.

* *Neo-Sannyasi* - see Sannyasi

* *Ribhu Gita*: one of the Vedantic poetic songs of India.

* *Sadhana*: Sanskrit, approx. Means to attainment. Spiritual practice. e.g. Meditation.

* *Samadhi*: Sanskrit, lit. 'firmly establish'. Supranormal stages of consciousness e.g. total absorption in the absolute or god or any object of awareness. Nirvakalpa Samadhi is the highest state of consciousness. Samadhi shrine - a commemorative burial place or tomb of a Great One.

* *Sannyasi:* one who renounces the world and all possessions to gain liberation. The term has been bastardized in contemporary usage. *Neo-Sannyasi* -new style of sannyasa created by Rajneesh for his followers. Neo-Sannyasi is the opposite of

222

the traditional form being partly characterized by
unrestrained sexual and psycho-spiritual experimentation.

* *Satchidananda*: Sanskrit, lit. 'Being-Consciousness-
Bliss'.an attribute of the absolute Brahman apperceived beyond words.

* *Satsang*: Sanskrit, lit. 'true or good company' Being in
the company of the holy man.

* *Shakti*: Sanskrit, lit. 'energy, power' Lord Shiva's consort.
The dynamic and personified aspect of godhead often linked
with the concept of Kundalini. Shakti - agency through
which creation sustenance and dissolution takes place.

* *Shaktipat*: Sanskrit. The giving of shakti. The transmission
of this potent energy from Guru to disciple. See Shakti.

* *Shiva*: Sanskrit, lit. the friendly or kindly one. Sometimes
refers to the supreme reality or the aspect of God that dissolves the universe and/or ignorance. The name *Shiva* has
multifarious applications.

* *Siddha*: Sanskrit, lit. 'complete, perfect'. It refers to the
perfected spiritual master, liberated and at one with God.

* *Skanda Puranas*: ancient Hindu devotional narratives-
scriptures.

* *Sufi*: *Sufi* Order - A form of Islamic mysticism.

* *Swami*: Sanskrit, lit. 'Sir'. A title of respect. Often refers to
Hindu celibate monks who renounce the world for God.

* *Vibhuti*: Sanskrit, lit. 'power'. Commonly refers to grey
ash produced by such power or ability.

* *Vedanta*: Sanskrit, lit. 'end of the Vedas'. A body of profound insights and 'prescriptions' regards the nature of life,
the Absolute and the right use of awareness to 'attain' liberation. *Vedanta* had a profound influence on the Hindu framework of thinking. *Vedanta* postulates the idea, that life as we
know it, is a mere apparency or illusion (maya).

* *Yatra*: Sanskrit, lit. 'procession or festivity'. Often refers to
religious excursion or festival.

* *Yoga*: Sanskrit, lit. 'yoke'. It commonly refers to being
yoked to or being united to God. There are over fourteen classical yogic paths to God in India. The Siddha Yoga of Swami
Muktananda, refers to the union with God (Yoga) that takes
place through the grace of the perfected master (Siddha).

The Experience Of Ultimate Truth

and other great books and biographies published by OM Books,
are available on retail and wholesale basis at the following address:

OM Books

P. O. Box 2190, Secunderabad 50003, A.P., India.
Street Address: OM Books, Logos Bhavan, Medchal Road
Jeedimetla Village, Secunderabad 500 055, A. P., India.

Phone: (040)-27861151, 27861152 Fax: (040)-27863956, 27861457
email: sales@omb.ind.om.org, (or) ombooks@satyam.net.in
Internet website: http://www.omegamusicindia.com or http://www.ombooks.org

Other Useful Biographies

Martin Luther	69.00	Jim Elliot	69.00
D. L. Moody	69.00	Sadhu Sundar Singh	60.00
Pioneers of Faith	69.00	Smith Wigglesworth	50.00
Amy Carmichael	55.00	Billy Graham	69.00
Charles Spurgeon	69.00	Through Gates Of Splendor	79.00